CISSP

A Comprehensive Beginners Guide on the Information Systems Security

Disclaimer

Knowledge and practices in this field changes constantly. As new experience and research widens our understanding, it may become important to make changes in professional practices, research methods, or medical treatment.

Researchers and practitioners must always depend on their own knowledge and experience in assessing and making use of any methods, data, experiments, or compounds, described in this book. In making use of such methods or information, they should mind their safety and that of others, who they are professionally responsible for.

Within the limits of the law, the authors doesn't take responsibility for damage and/or injury to property or persons whether through products negligence or liability, or from the application of any methods, instructions, or products in this book.

Table of Contents

Chapter One

Security Risk Management

As information security professionals, risk evaluation and mitigation are the key parts of our job. Dealing with risk is the theme of our roles, be it as firewall engineers, auditors, penetration testers, management, etc.

The key functions of the Security and Risk Management domain are risk analysis and mitigation as well as ensuring the best organizational structure for a robust information security system is in place. In this area of expertise, it's the quality of the people that can make or break an organization. By "quality of the people", we mean knowledgeable and experienced staff with supportive as well as vested leadership are of the highest quality.

Cornerstone Information Security Concepts

Information security is build on the foundation of these three concepts.

Confidentiality, integrity, and availability are popularly called the CIA triad.[1] The CIA acronym will be used in this book.

---

[1] Grasdal, M. (2017). Microsoft® U.S. National Security Team White Paper. Retrieved from http://download.microsoft.com/download/d/3/6/d36a0a81-6aa8-4ff4-835e-9a017df1f036/SecureCollaborationForProfSvcFirms.doc

Confidentiality. This prevents unauthorized read access to private data, and such confidentiality attacks can be theft of personally identifiable information (PII).

Integrity. This prevents unauthorized write access to data.

Availability. This ensures that data is accessible for regular business use.

Disclosure, alteration, and destruction. Disclosure is the unauthorized release of information. Alteration is the unauthorized alteration of data. Destruction is the process of rendering data or systems unavailable.

Identify and authentication. Identify on its own, is a claim. Authentication is done by supplying a collection of information only you possess. This can be a password or a passport.

Authorization. This is the set of actions carried out once identification and authentication has been done. It may be reading, writing, or executing files or programs.

Accountability. Accountability seeks to hold users responsible for the actions they take. Enforcing accountability keeps people sincere in their actions. Accountability itself is usually done by logging and carrying out data audit analysis.

Nonrepudiation. Nonrepudiation means a user cannot deny to have performed a specific transaction. Integrity and authentication are needed for nonrepudiation to occur.

Least Privilege and Need to Know. In least privilege, only a limited access of the needed access is granted to users to means users to get their job done.

Need to know means the user is required to know the specific information before accessing it.

Subjects And Objects. A subject is an active entity within a data system. Subjects can be people accessing data and can also be a computer program with access to the database.

An object on the other is passive and cannot manipulate other subjects within the database. Examples are documents on physical paper and text files.

Defense in Depth. Defense in depth is also called layered defense. It involves the use of multiple safeguards to protect an asset and improve its information security.

Legal and Regulatory Issues. In order to avoid legal issues surrounding information systems, data, and applications, information security professionals need to understand the concepts described in the next section.

Compliance with Laws and Regulations. This is a priority for both information security management and organizations. Knowledge of the law is essential so as not to break the law.

Major Legal Systems

In today's global economy, understanding common legal concepts and major legal systems is a necessity. Legal systems provide the framework upon which information system laws are built. Civil, common, and religious law forms the world's major legal systems.

Civil Law: This is the standard, major legal frameworks in many countries. This law uses codified laws and statutes to establish the limits of the law. Here, the legislature makes the law, and the judiciary interprets the law.

Common Law: This is the legal system used in most former British colonies and the United Kingdom.

Religious and Customary Law: Here, religious doctrine serves as the primary source of legal statutes and interpretation. Amongst the prominent religions, Islam is the most widespread source of religious legal systems, for example, the Sharia law system.

Customary Law: This legal system is characterized by the prevalence of widely accepted customs within a group. These customs are treated as laws and over time, may be formally made into law in a more traditional sense.

Criminal, Civil and Administrative Law

Within the common law, there are various branches.

Criminal Law: Crimes against individuals and in a broader sense, society are punished under criminal law. Criminal law is used to promote as well as maintain an upright citizenry by punishing offenders. In criminal cases, the burden of proof must be beyond reasonable doubt.

Civil Law: This is a major legal system in the world, and it's associated with the common law legal system. Tort law is the largest source of lawsuits seeking damages which result from an individual's negligence of duty.

Administrative Law: Administrative (or regulatory) law are compliance measures mandated by the government, and enacted by the executive arm of the government in the US. Examples include FCC regulations, FDA regulations, and FAA regulations.

Liability

The modern day society is a litigious one and negligence can be quite costly. As a result of this, legal liability is a fundamental concept for information security professionals as well as their employers.

Two important terms for corporate liability determination in the law court include due care and due diligence.

Due Care and Due Diligence

Due care which is also referred to as "prudent man" rule, means doing should be done by a logical person in any situation. Due diligence is the management of due care. An illustration that depicts the two concepts is: your staff patching their systems is due care, while verifying whether such action has been carried out is due diligence.

Gross negligence: This is a situation whereby the victim doesn't demonstrate due care. For example, if you lose PII and didn't protect your data, you have acted with gross negligence.

Legal Aspects of Investigations

Evidence: This is an important concept for information security professionals to understand as they often have to handle evidence during investigations.

Best evidence rule

Generally, original documents and tangible objects are more concrete as evidence as opposed to copies and oral testimony respectively. The best evidence should always be produced in court.

Evidence integrity: The best evidence is one that is reliable. Throughout forensic investigations, digital data is handled, and checksums are needed to ensure data hasn't been tampered with.

Entrapment and enticement: These are very similar in that both may involve law enforcement agencies. The difference is that in entrapment, an individual is persuaded to commit a crime by law enforcement agents while in enticement, only favorable conditions for the crime are provided.

Computer Crime

Computer crime is a crucial aspect of the interaction of legal system and information security. Computer crime laws vary across regional jurisdictions, but some generalities exist.

Intellectual Property

This refers to intangible property created through the mental effort of individual intellectual property concepts can give a competitive advantage to their owners.

Trademarks: These allow a brand to distinguish its source of products and services from others. Names, symbols, logos, and images are commonly trademarked items. The circled R symbol indicates a fully registered mark (trademark).

Patent: Patent provides the holder with exclusive rights to make or sell a novel and unique invention. The patent holder can prevent competitors from using their invention while the patent is still valid. Generally, a patent is valid for 20 years in Europe and the US.

Copyright: This is denoted by the circled c symbol, and it protects musical or literary works. Copyright protect from unauthorized modification and distribution.

Licenses: Software licenses are contracts between the software provider and the consumer. They may provide permission to the consumer to use the software as they deem fit or they may come with some restrictions. EULA (end-user license agreements) is unique because using the software provided constitutes a contractual agreement.

Trade secrets: This is information that is necessary to keep a business competitive. Due care and diligence are key to handling trade secrets. Protection methods commonly used are noncompete and nondisclosure agreements.

Privacy

This is the act of protecting host users PII confidentiality.

European Union Privacy: When it comes to business, the EU has a pro-privacy stance. Standardization of regulations on data privacy has a positive effect on commerce within the union and this is achieved through the EU Data Protection Directive.

OECD Privacy Guidelines: The Organization for Economic Co-operation and Development (OECD) consists of 30 member nations and during its forums, nations focus on global economic issues and issue consensus recommendations pertaining to policy changes within the association.

EU-US Safe Harbor: This was established to give US-based organizations the necessary framework required to handle data coming from the EU adequately. Participants (organizations) must adhere to the stricter data privacy principles in the EU Data Protection Directive.

International Cooperation

The most significant act of international cooperation in computer crime policy is the treaty put forward by the Council of Europe Convention on Cybercrime, a treaty also signed and ratified by the US. The major aim of the treaty is to standardize the cybercrime policy (investigation and prosecution) among the participating nations

Import/Export Restrictions

Many countries have moved to restrict import and/or export of cryptosystems and cryptographic hardware. This was done because these countries want their citizens to use cryptosystems their intelligence agencies can crack.

The Coordinating Committee for Multilateral Export Controls (CoCom), was a multinational agreement that was formed during the Cold War. It restricted the export of certain cryptographic technologies to Communist countries. After the war, the less restrictive Wassenaar Arrangement took its place, although export to non-member nations is still significantly limited.

Security and Third Parties

In recent years, the extent to which organizations rely on third parties to provide significant business services has increased the importance of an organization's information security department.

Service Provider Contractual Security

Contracts are the main security controls when dealing with third-party organizations. This is important given the trend of increased outsourcing.

Service Level Agreements (SLA): These are put in place to identify key expectations the vendor is contractually expected to meet. SLAs generally serve security purposes.

Attestation: This involves having a third party organization review the practices of the service provider. The statement produced from this review provides evidence as to whether the organization can be trusted or not.

Right to penetration test/right to audit documents: These provide written approval to the originating organization (or a trusted provider) to perform their own testing

A third-party audit or a penetration test conducted by the service provider can replace the aforementioned documents.

Procurement

This is the act of purchasing product and services offered by a third party. Utilizing the security department allows the organization to make risk-based decisions prior to vendor acceptance.

Vendor Governance

This is to ensure the service rendered by the third party provider to the business are usually of the appropriate standard. As this involves both sides, professionals are employed by the service provider and the company.

Acquisitions

Acquisitions can disrupt and affect aspects of the businesses involved especially in terms of information security.

Vulnerability assessment of the acquired company and penetration testing of networks form a key part of due diligence in this regard.

Divestitures

These are also known as demergers and deacquisitions. Here, a unified company breaks up into two or more. Divestitures come with more risks than acquisitions because failure to update old passwords and replace physical security controls(keys and badges) opens the new companies up to insider IT attacks.

Ethics

Ethics is the practice of doing what is morally right. An example of a code of ethics is the Hippocratic Oath, taken by doctors. Ethics is very important to information security professionals because we handle sensitive information and interact with customers, and in addition, our partners need to know that we will act with integrity.

The (ISC)2® Code of Ethics

This code of ethics is the most testable of such in the exams. Among other steps, agreeing to the code is crucial to becoming a CISSP®. The (ISC)2® code of ethics is available on the following website: https://www.isc2.org/ethics/default.aspx.

The code includes a preamble that serves as the introduction, mandatory canons, and advisory guidance.

Computer Ethics Institute

Another code of ethics to note are the Ten Commandments of Computer Ethics, put forward by the Computer Ethics Institute. The code is similar in format to the Ten Commandments of some of the world's major religions.[2] They are:

1. Thou shalt not harm others using a computer.

2. Thou shalt not interrupt the computer work of others.

3. Thou shalt not invade the privacy of other computer files.

4. Thou shalt not use a computer to bear false witness

5. Thou shalt not steal making use of a computer.

---

[2] The Computer Ethics Institute. "The 10 Commandments of Computer Ethics." CEI Online. 1992. Accessed 4 March 2019 from www.brook.edu/its/cei/overview/Ten_Commanments_of_Computer_Ethics.htm.

6. Thou shalt not use software that has not been paid for.

7. Thou shalt not try it gain unauthorized access to other people's computer resources.

8. Thou shalt not take credit for the intellectual output of other people.

9. Thou shalt consider social consequences when creating a program.

10. Thou shalt use computers in a considerate and respectable way.

IAB'S Ethics and The Internet

The Internet Activities Board (IAB) code of ethics is an RFC document(RFC 1087, Ethics and the Internet) published in 1987. According to the IAB when the following practices are carried out deliberately, they are regarded as unethical:[3]

1. Attempt to use internet resources without authorization

2. Disrupts the internet's intended use

3. Wastes resources of the internet

4. Destroys the integrity of computer-based information

5. Compromises privacy of users

---

[3] Wilson, S. (2007). The FCC Hearing at Stanford. *Legal Research Paper Series, 21.* Retrieved from https://law.stanford.edu/wp-content/uploads/2015/07/wilsons-rp21.pdf

Information Security Governance

This refers to all the activities carried out by an organization's senior management to ensure an adequate and successful information security system is in place with the organization.

Security Policy and Related Documents

Realistic as well as relevant policies are integral to any information security program. [4]These documents should be in line with the current times and should serve as a framework for the best way of doing things within the organization.

Policy: Policies are general, high-level management directives which are also mandatory.

Procedures: Unlike policies, procedures are low level and very specific guides to carrying out a given task. Procedures are also mandatory.

Standards: This describes the specific use of technology, and this applies to both hardware and software. A hardware standard might be listing the system requirements for a company laptop. A software standard can be specifying the brand and version of operating systems to be used on the laptop.

Standards are mandatory. They also lower a safeguard's TCO and they support disaster recovery.

---

[4] Information Security Chapter 5 Flashcards | Quizlet. (2019). Retrieved from https://quizlet.com/37179514/information-security-chapter-5-flash-cards/

Guidelines: Guidelines are discretionary recommendations that can also be seen as useful advice. An example can be a guide on how to create a strong password.

Baselines: Baselines are consistent ways of standard implementation. Baselines are also discretionary. One may decide to achieve a given goal without following the benchmarks of a baseline but they must produce comparable results to those that followed the standard. Senior management authorization is required for formal exception to baseline.

Personnel Security

An organization's biggest security risk can come from its users. As such, users should be properly trained and made aware of these risks. Background checks are also very crucial.

Security awareness and training: Security awareness involves bringing users' attention to key areas. Security training is the process of providing users and professionals with a skill set that'll improve their ability to interact with the information security systems.

Background checks: Background checks involve verification of criminal records (if any) as well of documents that provide information on an individual's certifications, education, and work experience. It is a key part of the hiring process.

Employee termination: This is a fair and legal process that involves revoking all forms of an employee's access. It has to carried out in a fair manner to avoid making a potentially dangerous enemy out of the former employee.

Vendor, consultant, and contractor security: These third parties can pose a security risk to the organization because of the possibility of accessing sensitive data. This risk, however, can be mitigated by proper security awareness, training of third party personnel as well as carrying out background checks. The information security policies, guidelines, and policies of the organization should also apply to them.

Outsourcing and offshoring: Both of these involve third parties providing IT services to an organization - they can lower the organization's TCO while enhancing its IT capabilities. The difference is the services provided in offshoring come from another country. Offshoring can present privacy issues because of the varying privacy laws that apply to various countries. A means of protecting offshored data is to seek legal counsel before entering such an arrangement and ensuring a contract is in place to offer guidelines as to how data will be handled in the other country.

Access Control Defensive Categories and Types

Here, each of the access controls will be discussed.

Preventive. Preventive controls are put in place to restrict what an authorized or unauthorized user can do.

Detective. Detective controls such as intrusion detection system are designed to act as alarms during attacks.

Corrective. Corrective controls focus on repairing a system or process that is been damaged. They work hand in hand with detective control. For example, an antivirus software would initially run a scan (detective) and quarantine or delete infected files (corrective).

Recovery. Recovery controls serve to restore system functionality after a security incident has occurred. For example, reinstalling an OS or recovering documents from backup.

Deterrent. Deterrent controls serves as a sanction that allows users to understand the consequences of illegal actions. For example, policies that state an employee will face termination if caught accessing illegal websites.

Compensating. This control acts to augment the weakness of other access controls.

Risk Analysis

For an information security professional, proper risk analysis is crucial as it determines the safeguards we deploy as well as the resources used to do so. Poor analysis can lead to wasted resources and compromised data.

Assets

Assets are resources that have been determined to need protection and their value, as assets determine the safeguards deployed towards their protection.

Threats and Vulnerabilities

A threat is an occurrence that can inflict damage.

A vulnerability is a feature that predisposes an entity to threat that can cause harm.

Risk = Threat × Vulnerability

Threats must connect to vulnerability for there to be risk. The formula for this is: Risk = Threat x Vulnerability

Values (numbers) can be assigned to specific risks when the formula is being used.

Impact

The Risk = Threat × Vulnerability equation can have the variable "Impact" added to it.

Risk = Threat × Vulnerability × Impact. Impact refers to the extent of damage, and it's expressed in dollars. Cost can replace Impact in the above equation.

Risk Analysis Matrix

A risk analysis matrix is a qualitative risk analysis that classifies risks based on the occurrence likelihood and their consequences. According to the matrix, there are low, medium, high, and extreme risks.

Calculating Annualized Loss Expectancy (ALE)

The ALE calculation helps in the determination of the annual cost of a loss associated with a given risk.

Asset value: This refers to the value of the asset to be protected.

There are three methods of computing intangible asset value according to Deloitte. They are:[5]

- **Market approach:** Here, it is assumed the fair asset value is the price of comparable assets purchased under similar conditions.

- **Income approach:** This approach focuses on the present value of an asset's future earning capacity.

- **Cost approach:** Here, the fair value of an asset is calculated in relation to the replacement cost of such asset.

EF (Exposure factor): This is the percentage loss in an asset's value due to an accident.

SLE (Single loss expectancy): This is a single loss cost.

ARO (Annual rate of occurrence): This refers to the number of such losses that occur each year.

ALE (Annualized loss expectancy): This is the cost incurred per annum due to risk. Its formula is SLE x ARO.

Total Cost of Ownership

The total cost of a reducing safeguard is the TCO. For example, the upfront cost for laptop encryption software is $100/laptop. A support fee of 10% is charged annually by the vendor. It is estimated that it would take 4 hours to install software on each laptop at a cost of $50

---

[5] Information Security Risk Management. (2019). Retrieved from http://isoconsultantpune.com/information-security-risk-management/

per hour plus benefits, and $70 including benefits. If this is carried out on 1000 laptops on a 3-year technology refresh cycle, the TCO over the 3 years would be calculated as:

Software cost: $100,000

Vendor support: $10,000 × 3 = $30,000

Staff cost per hour: $280,000

TCO for 3 years: $410,000

TCO per year: $410,000/3 = $136,667

Hence TCO for laptop encryption project is $136,667 per year.

Return On Investment

The amount of money saved by applying a safeguard is the ROI. You can have a positive ROI through your safeguard implementation, which can give you a lower annual TCO than ALE.

When an unencrypted laptop is stolen, the EF is 100% for both hardware and exposed data. Encryption reduces the PII exposure risk hence lowering EF to 10% for just hardware.

If the annual TCO of laptop encryption is $136,667 and ALE for a lost unencrypted laptop is $275,000, EF reduces ALE from $275,000 to $27,500 when encrypted. $247,500 is saved per year by incurring a TCO of $136,667. A positive ROI of $110,833 ($247,500 minus $136,667) is then made per year.

Budget and Metrics

Proper budgeting requires TCO and ROI calculations as well as risk analysis.

Risk Choices

After risk assessment, decisions must be made. The risk can be accepted, reduced, eliminated, transferred or avoided.

Accept the risk: In some cases, the cheapest option is to accept certain risks. Risks with low likelihood and consequences can be considered for acceptance while extreme risks should be avoided.

Mitigating (reducing) risk: In reduction analysis, risks are lowered to an acceptable level. The previous example of ALE on laptop encryption is a form of reducing risk. Sometimes, risks can be completely eliminated.

Transferring risk: There can be exchange of risk between entities as is done in the case of insurance companies

Risk avoidance: In extreme cases, avoiding risk is the best option when risk reduction is not possible. This conclusion is arrived at after thorough risk analysis.

Quantitative and Qualitative Risk Analysis

When doing risk analysis, these two methods are used. Hard metrics like dollar amounts (calculating the ALE) are used in analysing the risk quantitatively, while simple approximate values (the risk analysis matrix) are used in analysing risk qualitatively. Quantitative risk analysis is objective while qualitative risk analysis is subjective.

The Risk Management Process

The US National Institute of Standards and Technology (NIST) produced the guide on Risk Management for Information Technology Systems where it describes a nine-step risk analysis process:

- Characterization of Systems

- Identification of Threats

- Identification of Vulnerabilities

- Analyzation of Control

- Determination of Likelihood

- Analyzation of Impact

- Determination of Risk

- Recommendation of Control

- Documentation of Results

Types of Attackers

Information systems can be rendered vulnerable and attacked by the following attackers:

Hackers

Originally, hackers were known as non-malicious explorers who misuse technology.

Black hat hackers are malicious computer attackers.

White hat hackers work for the benefit of companies and institutions.

A hacktivist attacks computer systems for political reasons and this is known Hacktivism.

Script kiddies use tools which they have little understanding of, to attack computer systems.

Outsiders

Attackers with unauthorized access to a system are called outsiders.

Insiders

These are attackers who are internal users and have authorized access to the system. These attacks may be intentional or accidental.

Bots And Botnets

A computer system running malware is called a bot. They controlled via botnets

A botnet is a network managed by humans (bot-herders) which has central command and control over bots.

Phishers

A malicious attacker who tries to trick users and steal their PII is called a phisher.

The social engineering attack used by phisher is called phishing and this can involve the use of emails and websites that compromise clients when it's activated.

Chapter Two

Asset Security

In In this domain, we will discuss data classification and clearances, labels, ownership, and retention of data. We will also look at data remanence and remanence properties of SSDs. Lastly, controls determination will be discussed.

Classifying Data

Management of data classification methods is crucial to day to day access control management.

[6]Labels

Subjects have clearances while objects have labels. Many world governments use object labels like confidential, secret, and top secret.

Clearance

This is a formal determination of the trustworthiness of a user when provided access to a specific level of information.

---

[6] Information Asset and Security Classification Procedure - University of Southern Queensland. (2019). Retrieved from https://policy.usq.edu.au/documents/13931PL

Formal Access Approval

This is a documented approval issued by the owner of the data to the subject, granting them access to certain objects.

Need to Know

This is a general situation whereby a given computer system relies on least privilege and users only access information that they need to know.

Sensitive Information/Media Security

Sensitive Information: Every organization has sensitive information and steps must be taken to ensure such information is not destroyed, disclosed, or altered.

Handling: Due to their significant importance, sensitive information should have policies concerning how it is handled. People handling this information should be held accountable, and this is where policies are important.

Retention: Retention of sensitive information should not persist beyond their period of useful or legal requirement (whichever is greater). Retention beyond these periods exposes such information to disclosure threats.

Ownership

Owners of businesses, data, and systems as well as custodians and users have various responsibilities when it comes to information security

Business or Mission Owners

These owners ensure an organization's assets are properly secure.

Data Owners

They are responsible for how often data is backed up and labeling of sensitive data. They also perform management duties.

System Owner

This is a manager tasked with maintaining the security of the actual computers that house data.

Custodian

They provide services such as hands-on asset protection, and data restoration and backup. They follow the orders of data owners and deploy various solutions to meet targets set for them.

Users

They are required to adhere to policies, procedures, and standards. They must be aware of the penalties for failing to comply with such policies.

Data Controllers and Data Processors

Data controllers perform duties like data creation and management within a given organization. While data processors partake in data management on behalf of data controllers.

Data Collection Limitation

This is discussed in the OECD Collection Limitation Principle. It states that "Limits on the collection of personal data should be in place. Also, data should be obtained in a lawful manner and where applicable, with the owner's consent."

Remanence and Memory
Data Remanence

This is the residual data after noninvasive means have been used to delete it, especially forms of magnetic storage.

Memory

This is the on/off series of switches that represent bits. Memory may be tape based, chip-based, or disk based. The CPU memory has RAM and ROM components.

RAM and ROM: RAM is a volatile form of memory that holds instructions of currently running programs. It is volatile because a power loss can cause it to lose integrity.

ROM is nonvolatile and the computer BIOS is stored on it.

DRAM and SRAM: SRAM (Static Random Access Memory) makes use of small latches (flip flops) to store bits of information. DRAM (Dynamic Random Access Memory) is a cheaper and slower form of RAM. It stores bits in small capacitors that need constant refreshing to maintain integrity.

Firmware: A computer's BIOS or a router's operating system is stored on firmware because these programs don't change frequently. Firmware itself can be stored on various types of ROM like PROM, EPROM, and EEPROM.

Programmable Read-Only Memory (PROM) can only be written to once unlike erasable PROM (EPROM) and EEPROM that may be erased and written to multiple times.

EPROMs, EEPROMs, and flash memory are all programmable logic devices (PLDs) that can be programmed after leaving the factory.

Flash Memory: It's a unique type of EEPROM that is generally used as a device for storage as it can be written by large sectors.

Solid State Drives (SSD): This is a EEPROM + DRAM combination. They have logical blocks that are mapped to physical blocks, therefore, degaussing has no effect.

Garbage collection is a background process that identifies memory blocks that contain unneeded data and proceeds to clear such blocks during off-peak times.

The TRIM command makes invalid data and data that needs to be ignored. This makes garbage collection more efficient. It is an attribute of the ATA Data Set Management Command, and it doesn't reliably destroy data.

ATA Secure Erase is a process whereby physically undamaged data on SSDs are securely removed. Another process that achieves the same result is destruction.

Data Destruction

Object reuse is the unauthorized recovering of information from previously used forms of media. It can be prevented by securely cleaning and destroying objects before disposal.

Overwriting

This is the act of writing over every character of a file or in some cases, a disk drive. Overwriting is more secure than disk formatting.

Degaussing

This involves the destruction of a magnetic medium's integrity. It is done by exposing such a medium to a strong magnetic field.

Destruction

This is the process of physically damaging a media form's integrity.

Destructive measures can be shredding, incineration, and pulverizing. Destruction can also involve bathing metal components in a corrosive agent.

Destruction is more secure than overwriting.

Shredding

Shredding is a form of media sanitization and destruction that involves rendering hard copy data unrecoverable.

Determining Data Security Controls

Being able to determine appropriate data security controls is a very crucial skill. In order to choose and customize controls to be employed, standards, scoping, and tailoring should be utilized. Whether data is at rest or in motion is also a key determinant.

Certification and Accreditation

A system is certified when it meets the security requirements of the data owner. When a data owner accepts a certification and residual risk, accreditation is said to have occurred.

Standards and Control Frameworks

Various standards that help security control determination are available. We will discuss a few of these standards below

PCI-DSS. This is a security standard put forward by the Payment Card Industry Security Standards Council. Its aim is to protect credit cards by imposing security precautions on vendors.

The International Common Criteria. There's an International Common Criteria which is the internationally agreed upon standard for description and testing of IT security products. Within the common criteria, there are seven EALs that build upon the previous level.

ISO 17799 and the ISO 27000 Series. They (ISO) are a broad-based techniques and codes used in information security practise[7]

COBIT. This is a control framework that focuses on employing the best practices in the governance of information security. It was developed by the ISACA (Information Systems Audit and Control Association, see http://www.isaca.org)

ITIL®. This is also known as the Information Technology Infrastructure Library. As a framework, it provides the best services when it comes to IT management. It contains five Service Management Practices - Core Guidance publications available at: http://www.itil-officialsite.com:

- Service Strategy, which provides IT services

---

[7] von Solms, B. (2005). Information Security governance: COBIT or ISO 17799 or both?. *Computers & Security*, *24*(2), 99-104. doi: 10.1016/j.cose.2005.02.002

- Service Design, which details required infrastructure for IT services

- Service Transition, which describes new projects and makes them operational

- Service Operation, which covers IT Operations controls

- Continual Service Improvement, describes ways to improve existing IT services

Scoping and Tailoring

Scoping is the process by which segments of an organization's standard are determined.

Tailoring is the process by which a standard is adjusted to meet the needs of an organization.

Protecting Data in Motion and Data at Rest.

Data is said to be in motion when it is being transferred across a network. Data is at rest when it is stored and it resides on a disk or within a file.

Drive and tape encryption. This control is used in the protection of data after physical security breach has occurred. They protect data when it is at rest.

Media storage and transportation. It is important that sensitive data is backed up and stored offsite. The sites to be used in storing such should be secure and should follow strict procedures for data handling. It's best if an insured company is used for offsite transportation and storage of sensitive data.

Protecting data in motion. This form of data is best protected via standards-based end-to-end encryption such as IPSec VPN. VPNs may also be used as a defense in depth measure, especially for private corporate WAN.

Chapter Three

Security Engineering

In this domain, we'll discuss security architecture (security models, secure software, components), cryptography, and physical security.

Security Models

These provide rules that govern your operating system security. A good example of this is Bell LaPadula which includes "no read up" (NRU). This rule is also known as Simple Security Property, and it restricts a secret cleared subject from accessing a top-secret object.

Reading Down and Writing Up

Reading down is a situation whereby a subject reads a lower sensitivity object. Writing up is a situation whereby information is passed from an authorized subject to higher sensitivity object.

Bell - LaPadula Model

This focuses on maintaining object confidentiality. It was originally developed by the US Department of Defense.

Lattice-Based Access Controls

These are very useful as security controls in a complex environment. There are well defined upper and lower access limit for every subject and object relationship.

Integrity Model

While certain models concentrate on confidentiality rather than integrity, this issue is addressed by integrity models like Biba.

[8]**Biba Model.** Ensuring information integrity is protected is a major priority for most business. When it comes to integrity protection especially for time- and location-based information, Biba is the recommended model.

Clark Wilson. This real-world integrity model ensures integrity is protected by limiting the capability of subject. It does this by requiring subject to access object via programs.

Chinese Wall Model

Also known as the Brewer-Nash, it is designed to avoid conflict of interest. It does this by prohibiting an individual from accessing multiple conflict of interest categories.

Access Control Matrix

This is a table that defines access permission between specific object and subject. The roles applies to the subject's capability, while the column applies to the object capability.

---

[8] Conrad, E., Misenar, S., & Feldman, J. (2017). Domain 1. *Eleventh Hour CISSP®*, 1-32. doi: 10.1016/b978-0-12-811248-9.00001-2

Secure System Design Concepts

This design concept is the best universal practice and is of greater importance than specific hardware and software implementation.

Layering

This separates hardware and software functionality into modular tiers. And as such a change in one layer does not directly affect the other.

Abstraction

This hides unimportant information from the user. According to Bruce Schneier, "complexity is an enemy of security", i.e more complex processes are less secured.

Security Domains

This is a list of objects that a subject is permitted to access. They are more broadly defined as a group of subjects and objects that have similar security requirements.

Open and Closed Systems

An open system makes use of the open hardware made available by a variety of vendors. A closed system makes use of proprietary software and hardware.

Secure Hardware Architecture

Here, the focus is on the physical hardware necessary for a system to be secure.[9]

---

[9] https://docslide.us/education/syed-ubaid-ali-jafri-cissp-exam-guide-by-eric-conradseth-misenar.html

The CPU

This is the computer's brain, capable of performing complex and mathematical calculations. The number of clock cycles per second is used to rate a CPU's speed.

Arithmetic logic unit and control unit. The ALU is the part of the CPU that performs mathematical computations while control unit feeds the ALU with instructions.

Fetch and execute. This CPU process takes place in four steps:

- Fetch Instruction

- Decode Instruction

- Execute Instruction

- Write Result

All four steps are completed within one clock cycle.

Pipelining. This process combines multiple CPU steps into a single process and this allows for simultaneous executions of FDX cycles for different instructions. Pipelining makes a system more efficient because rather than having a CPU wait for an entire cycle before initiating another instruction, the CPU can work on different instructions in different stages of completion. Pipelining as a process increases CPU throughput.

Interrupts. Interrupts that occur in the CPU are hardware interrupts and can cause a CPU to halt the processing of a current task or save and initiate a new processing request, after which the old task is resumed.

Multiprocessing and multitasking. Multiprocessing, on the other hand, is a situation whereby multiple processes are run on multiple CPUs. Multitasking is the process whereby multiple tasks run simultaneously on a single CPU. Multiprocessing can be symmetric multiprocessing (SMP) where one operating system manages all CPUs or asymmetric multiprocessing (AMP), which has one CPU to one operating system.

Memory Protection

This is the requirement for secure multitasking systems as it stops a particular process from modifying the information security of other processes within the system.

Hardware segmentation. This acts as an advanced form of process isolation by mapping processes to specific locations.

Virtual memory. This facilitates multitasking, swapping, and other multiple processes by providing virtual address mapping between hardware memory and applications.

Swapping and paging. Swapping is the process by which virtual memory is used to copy contents of primary memory to secondary memory.

Basic input/output system. When the PC is turned on, the basic input/output system (BIO) executes the code contained in its firmware. It automatically runs a self-test to verify the integrity of BIO.

WORM storage. Write once, read many (WORM). Just as suggested by its name, it is used mostly for integrity assurance.

Trusted Platform Module (TPM)

This is a processor that provides additional security to hardware and ensures boot integrity.

The TPM chip is associated with full disk encryption implementation and hardware-based cryptographic operations

Data Execution Prevention (DEP) and Address Space Layout Randomization (ASLR)

These protect against attacks that exploit software vulnerabilities so as to obtain code execution capability. DEP prevents code execution, and ASLR makes exploitation more difficult.[10]

Virtualization and Distributed Computing

These have brought wholesale changes to applications, services, system data, and data centers.

Virtualization

This is a process whereby a software layer is put in place and it allows more than one operating system to run on one physical host computer simultaneously.

Hypervisor. This controls access between virtual guests and host hardware. A hypervisor can be Type 1 and Type 2. A Type 1 hypervisor is also called bare metal and it forms a part of the OS that

---

[10] Marco, H., Ripoll, I., de Andrés, D., & Ruiz, J. (2014). Security through Emulation-Based Processor Diversification. *Emerging Trends In ICT Security*, 335-357. doi: 10.1016/b978-0-12-411474-6.00021-9

runs on host hardware. Type 2 functions as an application on an operating system.

Virtualization security issues. The complexity of virtualization software makes it vulnerable. Vulnerability stems from multiple guests combining onto a single host. It's advisable that the guests combined have the same security requirements. A situation where an attacker exploits the host OS from another guest is called VMEscape.

Cloud Computing

The purpose of cloud computing is to enable large providers to leverage economies of scale to provide computing resources to other companies for fees. Cloud computing generally involves outsourcing IT infrastructure, storage, and applications to a third party.

The three commonly available levels of cloud provider service are Infrastructure as a service (IaaS) which provides only a virtualized system, Platform as a service (PaaS) which only provides a pre-configured operating system and Software as a service (SaaS) which is completely configured, from OS to applications.

A single organization, as well as entire governments, make use of the cloud because it reduces upfront capital expenditure, provides robust service levels, and reduces maintenance costs and leads to significant cost savings.

Cloud computing networks are vulnerable because the compromise of a single user can affect others. It's important to negotiate for the right to conduct vulnerability assessment and important penetration testing as well as the right to audit before signing a contract with a cloud computing provider

Grid- Computing

Grid computing is a process where computing ideas are shared to gain more computational results by people with different types of knowledge. Instead of high-performance computational needs like supercomputers, grid computing wants to control computational resources with different devices.

Large-Scale Parallel Data Systems

The aim of large-scale parallel systems is to increase performance using economies of scale. Its security concerns are to maintain data stored during work.

Thin Clients

They are central server-dependent, for serving and storage of data. It centralizes applications alongside their data, security, upgrade cost, patching, data storage, and more. It is dependent on software or hardware.

Peer-to-Peer Networks

Peer-to-Peer (P2P) networks affect the server computer model. Systems can perform as both client or server if data needed is provided. Also, decentralized peer-to-peer networks are dependable, because no central servers can be put offline.

System Vulnerabilities, Threats, and Countermeasures
Covert Channels

This is any communication that compromise security policy. For example, the malware communication channel installed on a system sees personally identifiable information (PII), and sends it to a harmful server.

Backdoors

A backdoor is a shortcut in a system used to bypass security verification to log in. Attackers install a backdoor after violating a system. Programmers and system designers install shortcuts in maintenance hooks which is a kind of backdoor for bypassing authentication.

Malicious Code

This is also referred to as malware. It is the general name for software that attack applications like, viruses, logic bombs, and Trojans, which can damage a system if affected, e.g zero-day exploits.[11]

Computer viruses. This is malware code that can't be used to spread a virus without a host (a file) and a carrier from one system to the other.

Worms. Worms are malware that spreads a virus independently. They cause damage using two ways: through malicious code in them and network failure.

Trojans. Also called Trojan horse malware functions in two ways: one is mild, i.e game, while the other is malicious. This term is derived from 'The Aeneid' - Virgil's poem.

Rootkits. These are malwares that changes some aspects of the operating system. User-mode rootkits work on most systems by

---

[11] Kabay, M. (2006). Introduction to Computer Crime. Retrieved from http://www.mekabay.com/overviews/crime.pdf

making use of ring-3, replacing some parts of the operating system in "userland" while a kernel-mode rootkits replaces parts of the operating system, but operates on ring-0.

Packers. Packers help to compress runtime of executables. The initial executable is reduced and a small decompressor is attached. When running, the decompressor removes the compressed executable machine before running it.

Logic bombs. This is a harmful program that reacts when a logical condition is reached, like after some transactions have been processed (otherwise called time bomb). Malware like worms contain logic bombs acting in a certain manner, and changing techniques on another time and date.

Client-Side Attacks

This results from downloading harmful content. Here running of data reverses compared to server-side attacks: client-side attack starts from the victim that downloads things from the attacker. [12]

Server-Side Attacks

Server-side attacks are launched from an attacker to the listening service; Patching, system hardening, firewalls are forms of defense-in-depth mitigate server-side attacks.

Web Architecture and Attacks

The previous World Wide Web was simpler. Most web pages were static, created in HTML (Hypertext Markup Language). The advent of

---

[12] Andress, J. (2011). *The basics of information security*. Waltham, MA: Syngress.

"Web 2.0," with powerful content, multimedia, and user-created data have added to the attack surface of the Web, giving it more attack vectors.

Applets. These are pieces of mobile embedded-in software like web browsers. It provides features that cannot be provide by HTML.

It is written in various programming languages; its two eminent languages are Java and ActiveX. The word "applet" is used for Java, while "control" is used for ActiveX, with the same functions.

Java. This is an object-oriented language used for popular programming language. Java platform-independent bytecode is interpreted using Java Virtual Machine (JVM). JVM to create operating systems like, Linux, FreeBSD, and Microsoft Windows.

Java applets run in a sandbox, which divides the code from the operating system.

ActiveX. ActiveX controls functions similarly to Java applets. They use digital certificates other than sandbox to provide security. ActiveX, a Microsoft technology works on Microsoft Windows operating systems only, unlike Java.

The Open Web Application Security Project (OWASP, see: http://www.owasp.org).

These application security resources provide a great ways of improving security conditions. Their most renowned project is the OWASP Top 10 project, which provides consensus guidance considered to be the top 10 most useful security applications. It is available at https://www.owasp.org/index.php/category/:OWASP_top_ten_project.

Extensible Markup Language. This is a markup language designed to encode documents and data, which is like HTML, but more universal in nature. It can be used on the web, to store application configuration and output from auditing tools, etc.

Service-Oriented Architecture (SOA). This service can be used by two or more organizations rather than individual application that needs the functionality offered by the service. It includes other common examples given to JavaScript Object Notation (JSON) used as basic structure of web services. SOAP (Simple Object Access Protocol) or REST (Representational State Transfer) provides connectivity, while the WSDL (Web Services Description Language) gives details on how to invoke the web services.

Database Security

A database presents different security challenges. The sheer amount of data stored in a database requires special security consideration. The users use collective measures to curb attacks through database security precautions.

Polyinstantiation. This makes it possible for two different objects to share same name.

Data mining. This is the process of sorting for millions of data to discover patterns and create relationships to tackle issues using data analysis. For example, credit card issuers have relied on data mining for searching tons of transactions stored in their databases to find out suspicious and fraudulent credit card activities.

Inference and aggregation. This happens if a user uses lower-level access to gain knowledge of restricted information.

Mobile Device Attacks

The latest security challenge is now on mobile attack, ranging from laptops to flash drives infected with malware due to lack of security. Traditional network-based protection are impotent in preventing the initial attack.

Cryptography

This is secret writing used to secure information sent to someone. Only the individual who knows the key can decrypt it. Third parties should remain oblivious of such information.

Key Terminologies

Cryptology helps to secure communication, while cryptography hides the content of the messages; cryptanalysis is the art of opening the encrypted information so as to understand their meaning. A plaintext is when a message is unencrypted, Cipher is a cryptographic algorithm, while Decryption converts ciphertext again into plaintext, and Encryption turns plaintext to Ciphertext.

Confidentiality, Integrity, Authentication, and Nonrepudiation

Cryptography works to ensure confidentiality and integrity; it doesn't directly provide availability. It can also provide authentication, which proves an identity claim.

Permutation, Substitution, Diffusion, and Confusion

For permutation, which is also called transposition, it provides diffusion by rearranging the characters of the plaintext, while substitution causes confusion by replacing characters.

Diffusion connotes that the orderliness of the plaintext must be dispersed in the ciphertext, and confusion states that the link between the plaintext and ciphertext must be made random.

Polyalphabetic and Monoalphabetic Ciphers

A polyalphabetic cipher deals with various alphabets substituting for a specific alphabet. For example, X substitutes for E on the first round, then substitutes for Z on the next round. While monoalphabetic cipher makes use of one alphabet to substitute for another.

Exclusive OR (XOR)

This is the propeller behind today's encryption. Joining a key and a plaintext using XOR helps to create a ciphertext. XOR using the same key with the ciphertext helps to create the original plaintext. It's easy and fast to solve the XOR math, so much that phone relay switches can be used in doing it.

Two bits are true (or 1) if one or the other is 1 (but never both). i.e. When two bits are the same, the answer is 0 (false) if they are different, the answer is 1 (true). [13]

Data in Motion and Data at Rest

Here, cryptography helps to protect both of them.

Whole disk encryption of a magnetic disk drive or full disk encryption uses software like PGP or BitLocker. While Whole Disk Encryption is a form of encrypting data at rest, SSL or IPsec VPN are examples of encrypting data in motion.

---

[13] The XOR Cipher - HackThis!!. (2019). Retrieved from https://www.hackthis.co.uk/articles/the-xor-cipher

Protocol Governance

This describes the steps taken in selecting the best technique and implementation for the right job, basically on an organization-wide scale. For example, symmetric ciphers are mainly used for confidentiality, and AES is preferred over DES due to its strength and performance, while a digital signature helps with authentication and integrity, but not with confidentiality.

Types of Cryptography

Symmetric Encryption

This uses the same key for decrypting and encrypting files. When you decrypt and encrypt zip files using one key, you are said to be using symmetric encryption. Symmetric encryption is also known as "secret key" encryption.

Stream and Block Ciphers. In stream mode, each bit is encrypted independently in a "stream," while the encrypt blocks of data is ciphered in each round in block mode

Initialization Vectors and Chaining. Most symmetric ciphers make use of an initialization vector in encrypting block of data and ensuring it is random.

In chaining, the previous encrypted block is seeded into the next block for encryption, negatively affecting the resulting patterns in the ciphertext.

DES. DES means data encryption standard. It details the DEA, which is Data Encryption Algorithm. IBM designed DES based on their older

Lucifer symmetric cipher, which uses a 56-bit key and 64-bit block size (ie, it encrypts 64 bits each round).[14]

RC5 and RC6. RC5 uses 128-bit blocks, 64-bit (to replace DES), or 32-bit (for testing purposes). Keys range in size from zero to 2040 bits.

RC6 is build on RC5 framework, and is modified to match the requirements of AES. Also, it has more strength than RC5. It encrypts 128-bit blocks making use of 192-, or 128-, 256-bit keys.

Twofish and Blowfish. The creator of Applied Cryptography, Bruce Schneider, created the two symmetric, Two-fish and block ciphers Blowfish.

Twofish is an AES finalist, using 128-bit through 256-bit keys to encrypt 128-bit blocks, while Blowfish goes from 32- through 448-bit keys in encrypting 64 bits of data. They are both open algorithms; that is, they are freely available.

Asymmetric Encryption. This makes use of two different keys in decrypting and encrypting files. The public key is also called asymmetric encryption. For any two persons to exchange communication, the receiver needs to download the sender's posted public key which will help them encrypt their plaintext.

Asymmetric Methods. Math relies on asymmetric progress. In these methods, direct functions are used, easier to compute in one direction but not easy to compute in the other direction.

---

[14] Common Cryptographic Algorithms. (2019). Retrieved from http://web.deu.edu.tr/doc/oreily/networking/puis/ch06_04.htm

Discrete Logarithm. Logarithm is the contrary form of exponentiation. Computing 7 to the 13th power (exponentiation)- is easy using today's calculator: 96,889,010,407. Asking the -question "96,889,010,407 is 7 to what power," meaning the logarithm is more difficult. Discrete logarithms apply logarithms to groups, it's a more difficult problem to solve.

Factoring Prime Numbers. One way to apply direct function is to factor composite numbers into their primes. When you multiply two prime numbers, 6,269 by 7,883, the answer showed in the composite value is 49,418,527.[15]

This calculation is termed factoring, and has been the only existing way for many years.

Diffie-Hellman Key Agreement Protocol. Key agreement gives two parties the security to agree on a symmetric key through a public channel, like the internet. An intruder able to sniff the entire conversation cannot derive the exchanged key. Martin Hellman and Whitfield Diffie created the Diffie-Hellman Key or Exchange Key Agreement Protocol in 1976.

Elliptic Curve Cryptography. ECC manipulates a direct function that uses separate logarithms as done to elliptic curves. This is harder to solve than solving discrete logarithms, meaning algorithms centered on elliptic curve cryptography (ECC) are more rigid per bit than systems using discrete logarithms.

---

[15] Downnard, I. (2002). Public-key cryptography extensions into Kerberos. IEEE Potentials, 21(5), 30-34. doi: 10.1109/mp.2002.1166623

Symmetric Tradeoffs and Asymmetric. This asymmetric encryption is far weaker and slower per key length bit than symmetric encryption. The aim of asymmetric encryption is to communicate securely without presharing a key.

Hash Functions

This function enables encryption through the use of algorithm without a key. The encryption can't be reversed, therefore, they are referred to as one-way (hash) functions.

MD5. Message-Digest algorithm 5 is one of the highest used hash algorithms in the MD class. It creates hash value of 128-bit on any length of input. MD5 has been widely known over the years, but there are various problems associated with it where collisions is found in a given period of time.

Collisions. Here, no hash is unique as the number of specific hash is lower than the number of possible plaintexts.

Secure Hash Algorithm (SHA). This is what a hash algorithm series is called. 160-bit hash value is created by SHA-1. SHA-2 includes SHA-512, -384, -256, and -224; they are named according to the message-digest length each creates.

Cryptographic Attacks

Cryptanalysts use cryptographic attacks to gain the plaintext without using a key.

Brute Force

In this kind of attack, the entire possible keyspace is generated, but the plaintext will be recovered if given enough time.

Social Engineering

This uses the mind to bypass security controls; it can recover a key by tricking the holder into revealing it. Techniques are varied; one is to impersonate an authorized user.

Known Plaintext

This attack recovers and analyses a ciphertext pair and matching plaintext; its target is to get the used key. The reason the key is needed even when you have the plaintext is because other ciphertexts encrypted with same key can be decrypted by the key.

Adaptive Chosen Ciphertext and Chosen Ciphertext

This chosen ciphertext and plaintext attack one mirror. Here, the cryptanalyst selects the ciphertext to be decrypted on its own. This ciphertext is then launched against cryptosystems that are asymmetric, with the cryptanalyst choosing which public documents to decrypt with the user's key.

However, adaptive-chosen ciphertext mirrors its plaintext cousin by starting with a defined ciphertext attack in the first round, and continuing based on the previous phase.

Adaptive Chosen Plaintext and Chosen Plaintext

This cryptanalyst picks a plaintext to be encrypted in a particular attack so as to get the key. Encryption is done without knowledge of the key through an encryption oracle.

Adaptive-chosen plaintext starts with a preferred plaintext attack in the initial phase. Afterward, the cryptanalyst "adapts" and continues the encryption using the previous round.

Known Key

This term is confusing because the attack is done once the cryptanalyst identifies its key. That is, the cryptanalyst understands a bit of the key and uses it to reduce the attack towards the key.

Differential Cryptanalysis

This tries to locate the relationship between encrypted plaintexts that are related, and that which may be slightly different. This attack is initially launched as adaptive chosen plaintext attack

Linear Cryptanalysis

This plaintext attack is a popular one in which the same key is used to create cryptanalyst source for large quantity of plaintext or ciphertext pairs. Also, every pair is consciously studied to get information concerning the key that was used in creating them. The term differential linear analysis is used when both linear and differential analysis are combined.

Side-Channel Attacks

These attacks make use of physical data in opening cryptosystem, and power consumption or monitoring the cycles of CPU used while decrypting or encrypting.

Implementing Cryptography

Hash-based, asymmetric, and symmetric cryptography don't exist alone; instead, they have genuine applications which are mixed with each other and can provide integrity, confidentiality, nonrepudiation, and authentication.

Digital Signatures

They are used in signing cryptographic documents. They first provide nonrepudiation, then authenticate the signer's identity and integrity of proof of document, meaning that in the future, the document can't be denied to have been signed by the sender.

Public Key Infrastructure (PKI)

This influences all the known types of encryption helping in the management of digital certificates. This certificate is the public key assigned alongside digital signature. It could be client-based or server-based. [16]

Certificate authorities and organizational registration authorities. The CAs (Certificate Authorities) issue digital certificates. While the identity of a certificate holder is authenticated by the Organizational Registration Authorities (ORAs) before issuing to them, an organization may operate as a CA or ORA (or both).

Certificate revocation lists: This is maintained by the CAs. The CRL is a list of revoked certificates. If an employee gets fired or a private key goes missing, then a certificate is revoked. The Online Certificate Status Protocol (OCSP) is swapped with a CRL which scales better.

Key Management Issues. CAs distribute digital certificates to holders. During distribution, the integrity and confidentiality of the holder's private key must be guaranteed. Public/private key pairs used in PKI are stored centrally and securely in order not to lose their passwords.

---

[16] Syed Ubaid Ali jafri - CISSP Exam Guide by Eric Conrad,Seth Misenar. (2019). Retrieved from http://docslide.us/education/syed-ubaid-ali-jafri-cissp-exam-guide-by-eric-conradseth-misenar.html

There will be problems in cryptanalysis when a private key is lost, which could also lead to losing all files encrypted with the matching public key.

SSL and TLS

Transport Layer Security (TLS) is the successor to SSL and both are utilized as a part of Hypertext Transfer Protocol Secure (HTTPS).

SSL as a web browser was developed for Netscape in the 1990s.

IPsec

This Internet Protocol Security (IPsec) provides both the IPv4 and IPv6 with cryptographic layer. This techniques used in providing virtual private networks (VPN), and sending private data over networks that are insecure; Here, the data goes through the public network in a "virtually private" manner. The two main protocols provided by IPsec are Authentication Header (AH) and Encapsulating Security Payload (ESP).

AH and ESP. This, authentication header (AH), helps with integrity and authentication for various packets of network data. It assures no confidentiality and serves as a digital signature for the information. It protects against attacks, in a place where data is hindered from the network so as to reuse encrypted authentication credentials fraudulently. ESP on its own primarily aids confidentiality by encrypting packet data.

Security Association and ISAKMP. When communication is exchanged between two systems through ESP, it means they make use of two SAs, both for different paths. When AH is being leveraged together with ESP by the systems, two or more SAs are used. The

ISAKMP (Internet Security Association and Key Management Protocol) manages the SA creation process.

Tunnel and Transport Mode. This is where IPsec is used. Security gateways apply tunnel mode to ensure point-to-point tunnels for V.

Perimeter Defenses (IKE). This determines which algorithm to be selected from the many encryption algorithm used by IPsec including the Triple DES or AES for confidentiality, and MD5 or SHA-1 for integrity.

Pretty Good Privacy (PGP)

This was created by Phil Zimmerman in 1991, and brought asym-metric encryption to users. PGP provides today's suite of cryptography with the idea of integrity, nonrepudiation, confidentiality, and authentication.

S/MIME

MIME (Multipurpose Internet Mail Extensions) is an easy (or even the easiest) way of formatting an email with characters and sets, together with attachments. Secured MIME helps PKI in encrypting and authenticating a MIME-encoded email. The S/MIME gateway, which is the client email server, performs the encryption.

Escrowed Encryption

This is when a different organization has access to a copy of a public/private key. Which is often divided into parts, each escrow-held by a third-party before released.

Perimeter Defenses

This help to detect and control unauthorized physical access. Networks are used in buildings for thorough defenses. Individuals should endeavor to apply physical security controls to critical assets using doors, walls, and locks.

Fences

Fences may range from 3-foot/1-m tall fencing to 8-foot-tall (2.4 m) which are mainly wired with barbed wire on top of them. Also, fences should be designed to control the entering and exit of personnel, like gates and exterior doors.

Gates

These range from various classes. From the first class gate specifically designed against attackers, to the fourth class gate which is to prevent cars from going through entrances unchecked.

Lights

These include lights for both detective and deterrent control, used to see intruders. A type of light includes the Fresnel Light, which is named after Augustine-Jean Fresnel.

Measurement of light terms include lumen, which is the amount of light one candle creates.

Locks

These are security control components made for preventive efforts. It is used on doors and windows to prevent intruders gaining physical access to a building. It could be mechanical, like combination locks, or electronic locks, which are most times used with magnetic stripe cards or smart cards.

Combination Locks. These have dials which must be turned in a particular order to unlock. Some have buttons which also make use of numeric combinations.

Tailgating/Piggybacking

This is a situation in which an authorized person is followed into a building by an unauthorized person after the door was opened by the authorized person.

Motion Detectors and Other Perimeter Alarms

In security cases, both microwave and ultrasonic motion detectors are known to work well. For example, the Doppler Radar is used to predict the weather. Here, there's an echo when it hits an object and bounces off. Also, after there's emission of a energy wave, the echo goes back very fast if an object reflects the wave.

A light beam is sent to a photoelectric sensor by a photoelectric motion sensor over the space that is being monitored. When the light beam is broken, this same sensor is alerted.

Contraband Checks

These are used to identify objects banned from going through a secure area. They often detect weapons, metals, or explosives.

Doors and Windows

Strive to understand the weaknesses and strengths of windows, doors, floors, walls, and ceilings in order to avoid access from attackers. Exits must be free in the possibility of an emergency, and a simple door push or motion detectors should allow easy exiting. Emergency doors leading outside should be the best route marked for emergency.

Guards

These are powerful control agent in many situations. They can inspect and access credentials, act as a general deterrent, and monitor CCTV cameras and environmental controls.

Dogs

They provide defense duties in homes, most commonly in areas outside and near fences.

Site Selection, Design, and Configuration

Selection, design, and configuration are all involved in the process of building a well-equipped facility like a data center, from the site selection process to the final design.

[17]Site Selection Issues

Site selection is the greenfield process of selecting a site to build a data center. A greenfield is a plot of land yet to be developed. It has the design similar to a black canvas.

Utility Reliability. The strength and reliability of local utilities is a concern with site selection purposes. Electrical failures create the most common failures and disasters.

Uninterruptible power supply (UPS) provides protection against electrical failure for a period of time, and generators for an extended period, if refueled.

---

[17] Syed Ubaid Ali jafri - CISSP Exam Guide by Eric Conrad,Seth Misenar. (2019). Retrieved from http://docslide.us/education/syed-ubaid-ali-jafri-cissp-exam-guide-by-eric-conradseth-misenar.html

Crime. Local crime rates are a factor in site selection. The most important thing here is employee safety; all employees possess the right to a safe and healthy working environment.

Site Design and Configuration Issues

After selection, a lot of design decisions are made. Will the site be openly made a center for data? Are there any tenants sharing the building? Where should the telecom demarcation point be?

Site Marking. Most data centers are not openly marked so as not to bring people's attention to the facility and its expensive contents. A building with a proper design is an important in avoiding attackers.

Shared- Tenancy and Adjacent Buildings. Many other tenants living in the building could as well pose security issues, since they are already behind the physical security perimeter. Tenants careless attitude toward visitor security can endanger your security.

Shared Demarcation. The problem most people face in a shared building, is the pattern of its demarcation. This is where the Internet service provider (ISP) responsibility ends, leaving customers to take over the other responsibility of getting internet service. Today, buildings have a demarcation area and all external circuits are entered into the building. Access to it affects the confidentiality, integrity, and availability of the circuits and the data within them.

Media- Storage Facilities. Offline storage of media for recovery from disaster, potential legal proceedings, or regulatory purposes is normal. A media storage created away from the primary facility makes the data accessible even when there are physical problems at the primary facility.

System Defenses

This is one of the last in a thoroughly designated defense strategy. It tries to proffer solutions and curb attackers from having direct access to the device or media containing important information. In most cases when other controls may have failed, it stands out as the superior technique and remains the final phase in data protection.

Asset Tracking

Effective asset tracking databases empower physical security. You only protect your data when you know what and where it is. Detailed asset tracking databases conform with regulatory compliance by identifying where there is regulated data within a system using serial and model numbers.

Port Controls

This could become faulty due to large amounts of information stored in it. It can as well be turned off physically. Examples of port control ideas are disconnecting the internal wires connecting the port to the system, disabling ports on a system's motherboard, and physically obstructing the port itself.

Environmental Controls

These controls ensure a conducive environment for personnel and their equipment. Examples include power, HVAC, and fire safety.

Personnel Safety, Training, and Awareness

Personnel safety is the main goal of physical security. It offers the opportunity for the personnel to make use of an emergency power system.

Evacuation Routes. Post-evacuation routes should be in a prominent location, as they are in hotel rooms, for example. All visitors and personnel should be advised of the quickest evacuation route from where they are. Every site should designate a point where all personnel will meet in case of an emergency.

Evacuation Roles and Procedures. The major evacuation roles widely followed for safety are the meeting point leader and safety warden. The latter should ensure that all personnel safely and carefully leave the building in a situation of emergency, while the former assures that all personnel involved are accounted for at the emergency meeting point.

Duress Warning Systems. This type of warning is drafted to enable immediate signaling in the event of emergencies like chemical contamination, bad weather, threat of violence and so on.

Travel safety. Safety matters in all phases of business, both in authorized homes or abroad. Telecommuters should have the proper equipment, including ergonomically safe workstations, as business travel to certain areas may not be safe. When organizations like the US State Department Bureau of Consular Affairs issue travel warnings (http:// travel.state.gov/), it should be taken note of by personnel before traveling abroad.

ABCDK Fires and Suppression

Safe evacuation is the major safety issue for when there's a fire. Different types of fires have different suppressive agents requirements. These suppressive agents extinguish fires.[18]

The A-class include combustibles like wood and paper. This is very common. Extinguish this type of fire with water or soda acid.

B-class fires include burning oil, alcohol, gasoline, and other products of petroleum should be extinguished using gas or soda acid. Water should never be used to extinguish this class of fire.

C-class fires are fires ignited by electricity. It may ignite in wiring or equipment. They are conductive fires, and must be extinguished using a non-conductive agent, such as gas.

The D-class of fires involve burning metals; it is advisable to use dry powder to extinguish them.

The K-class are the kitchen fires, which involve burning grease and oil. Extinguishing this class involves the use of wet chemicals.

Fire Suppression Agents

These suppression tools work using four possible methods which could also be combined:

- they interfere with the chemical reaction taking place inside the fire

---

[18] Types of Fires and Extinguishing Agents – The Fire Equipment Manufacturers' Association. (2019). Retrieved from https://www.femalifesafety.org/types-of-fires.html

- they reduce the oxygen supply to the fire

- they reduce the fire's temperature.

Water. It extinguishes fire by suppressing the temperature lower than the ignition point. It is recommended to extinguish common combustibles. It is the safest suppressive agents.

Soda Acid. This is an older extinguishing technique that uses a mixture of sodium bicarbonate (soda) and water. A glass vessel of acid is suspended inside the extinguisher which is broken by an external lever.

Dry Powder. Using dry powder to extinguish a fire works by reducing the temperature, and eventually making the fire starved of oxygen. Metal fires can be extinguished this way. An example of dry powder is sodium chloride.

Wet Chemicals. Kitchen fires and common combustibles like paper and rubber are also extinguished using this method. The chemical content is made up of a mixture of water and potassium acetate.

CO_2. The risk in using CO_2 is that it is colorless and odorless, and will be breathed in by our bodies like air. Removing oxygen smothers fire in CO_2 fire suppression.

The risk involved in CO_2 is that it may cause suffocation because of lack of oxygen.

Sprinkler Systems. Here, the pipes (wet pipes or dry pipes) have sprinkler heads. But the wet pipes have water right up to the sprinkler heads and the dry pipes have compressed air. These pipes open up after being triggered by a fire alarm. Deluge systems release water using two separate ignitions. A preaction system is a combination of dry, wet, or deluge systems.

Halon and Halon Substitutes. They extinguish fire by making use of a chemical reaction which reduces the fire's temperature. The production and consumption of Halon was banned in developed countries as of Jan. 1, 1994 due to its depleting properties.

Portable fire extinguishers. These should be as small as possible for personal use, and must be identified by indicating the fire they should be used to extinguish on their containers.

Chapter Four

Communication

Communications and network security are essential in today's world. The internet, online banking, instant messaging, the world wide web, email, and other technologies depend on network security; our world today can't do without it.

Communications and network security centers on privacy, trustworthiness, and the availability of data in motion.

Communications and Network Security is among the biggest domains in the Common Body of Knowledge and has more concepts than other domains. It is also one of the domains that require practical knowledge about segments, frames, packets, and headers.

Network Architecture and Design

This first section will explain network configurations and control content, focusing on utilizing and comparing the price, benefits, and technicalities of network control.

Fundamental Network Concepts

Before we start, there is a need to understand the basic principles behind what we are about to study. Terminologies like broadband are most times applied informally; the exam demands a detailed comprehension of information security.

Simplex, Half-duplex, and Full-duplex Communication. Simplex communication is unidirectional, like a car radio. Half-duplex communication- information is transmitted/received just once, like a walkie-talkie. In full-duplex communication, information is transmitted/received simultaneously, like when you are having a conversation.

LANs, WANs, MANs, GANs, and PANs.

LAN - Local Area Network is a relatively small network within a building or in surrounding areas.

MAN - Metropolitan Area Network is restricted to a city, ZIP code, campus, or park. WAN - WAN defines a wide area network, usually covering cities, states, or countries.

GAN - GAN refers to a global area network, and is a global collection of WANs.

PAN - PAN covers the smallest distance (100 m or less); used by low-power wireless communications like Bluetooth.

Internet, Intranet, and Extranet. The Internet is a global system of interconnected network operating Transmission Control Protocols/Internet Protocols (TCP/IP), creating effective service. Intranet is privately operated TCP/IP, for example, an organization's network. However, Extranet is a interlink between Intranets, for example, a link to business partners.

Circuit-switched and Packet-switched Networks. Voice networks created in early times were circuit-switched whereby a channel or circuit (part of a circuit) was a file-server for two nodes. Point-to-point connections-like a T1 connecting two offices, can be done using circuit-switched networks.

A disadvantage of circuit-switched networks is connecting a channel or circuit makes it dedicated to that function only, even in the absence of data transfer. Packet-switched networks were devised to confront this issue and handle network failures more efficiently.

Rather than using dedicated circuits, packet-switched networks break data into packets, all sent individually. If multiple routes exist between two points on a network, packet switching chooses the best route and leans back on secondary routes in case of a failure. Packets could take any path across a network and are later reassembled by the receiving node. Lost packets can be retransmitted while out-of-order packets can be re-sequenced.

Contrarily, packet-switched networks, unlike circuit-switched networks, allows unused bandwidth to be used for other connections. This makes packet-switched networks a cheaper option.

Quality of service. Allowing unused bandwidth to be used for other connections poses a problem: what happens when the bandwidth is exhausted? Which type of connection gets the bandwidth? This isn't a problem with circuit-switched networks, where applications are entirely connected to dedicated circuits or channels.

Quality of service (QoS) is utilized by packet-switched networks to give precise traffic advantage over other traffic; QoS is used in Voice-over Internet protocol (VoIP) traffic (voice through packet-switched data networks) to stop interception of calls.

Simple Mail Transfer Protocol (SMTP), a store-and-forward protocol employed in emails, is not as sensitive to delays; interruptions in email exchange cannot be noticed as quickly as dropped calls.

The OSI Model

The Open System Interconnection model is a layered network model. This model is hypothetical; the OSI model is not implemented directly in systems (most systems now use the TCP/IP model). Instead, it is used as a reference point, so "Layer 1" (physical) is globally understood, even if you are running Ethernet or ATM, for instance. "Layer X" here refers to the OSI model.

[19]The OSI model has seven layers. From top-to-bottom:

Layer 1: Physical

Layer 1 represents units of data like bits, expressed by energy (like electricity, light, or radio waves) and the material of transmittance, like fiber optic cables or copper. WLANs has a physical layer, but cannot be touched.

In many devices, repeaters, and nubs, Layer 1 has cabling standards such as unshielded twisted pair (UTP), thicknet, and thinnet.

---

[19] The OSI Model – What It Is; Why It Matters; Why It Doesn't Matter. (2019). Retrieved from http://www.tech-faq.com/osi-model.html

Layer 2: Data link

Access to Layer 1 and LAN connection is controlled by Layer 2. The media access control (MAC) address, its ethernet card, as well as the bridges and switches stand at layer 2.

There are two other sLayer 2 consists of two other layers: logical like control (LLC) and media access control (MAC) which exchanges information between Layer 1, while LLC controls LAN connections (Layer 3)

Layer 3: Network

Routing (transmitting information across LANs on two different systems) represents Layer 3. It consists of routers and IP addresses.

Layer 4: Transport

Layer 4 controls sequencing of packet, control of flow, and detection of error. Protocols include UDP (User Datagram Protocol), and TCP (Transmission Control Protocol). It provides components like resending and resequencing packets. Protocol implementation determines the use of these components. TCP implements these components but is slower. UDP is faster as it doesn't utilize these components.

Layer 5: Session

Layer 5 controls sessions, which maintains connections. Sharing files across a network requires maintenance sessions, like remote procedure calls (RPCs) on Layer 5. The session layer enables communication between applications. It uses simplex, half-duplex, and full-duplex communication.

[20]Layer 6: Presentation

Data is presented to the application and user in an understandable manner by Layer 6. Characters like ASCII, image formats like TIFF (tagged image file format), GIF (graphics interchange format), and JPEG (joint photographic experts), and conversion of data, all occur in the presentation layer.

Layer 7: Application

Layer 7 allows the user to interface with the application. Instant messaging, word processing and web browsing occurs at this layer. Protocols include Protocols Telnet and FTP.

The TCP/IP Model

Its informal name is TCP/IP while its formal name is the Internet Protocol Suite.

Network access layer. Layers 1 (physical) and 2 (data link) of the OSI model are integrated by the TCP/IP model network access layer. It describes layer 1 components like energy, bits, and the transmittance material (wireless, fiber, copper). Problems in Layer 2 like changing bits into protocols like: Network Interface Cards (NICs), MAC addresses and ethernet frames are addressed.

Internet layer. The OSI model's layer 3 (network) is equivalent to the internet layer of the TCP/IP. IP addresses and routing occurs here. An internet layer is used to send information across nodes on different LANs. Protocols include routing protocol, IPv6, IPv4, ICMP, and others.

---

[20] The OSI Model – What It Is; Why It Matters; Why It Doesn't Matter. (2019). Retrieved from http://www.tech-faq.com/osi-model.html

Host-to-host transport layer. This is commonly referred to as "Transport"; it creates a connection between the application layer and internet layer. Here, ports are used to address application on a network.

Application layer. The TCP/IP integrates layers 5,6 and 7 of the OSI model. Majority of these protocols utilize a client-server configuration, where the user links to a server. The user and servers utilizes TCP, UDP, or both as their transport layer protocol. Secure shell (SSH), Telnet, and FTP are protocols of TCP/IP application-layer.

MAC addresses. The distinct hardware address of an Ethernet NIC is a MAC address, in-built from the factory. Software can be used to modify them.

EUI-64 MAC addresses. An extended unique identifier, 64-bit addresses was created by the IEEE. It enables more MAC addresses than 48-bit addresses. Both MAC addresses can be configured using IPv6.

IPv4t. IPv4 is connectionless and unreliable; it guarantees "best effort" packet delivery. When required, a high-level protocol (like TCP) provides reliability and connection.

IPv6. IPv6 is a modification of IPv4, with larger address spaces (IPv6 has 123-bit addresses, IPv4 has 32-bits), easier routing, and easier address assignment. IPv6 was created to correct the shortage of IPv4 addresses.

TCP. TCP is a layer 4 protocol that utilizes a three-way handshake to create connections across a network. TCP can rearrange segments that are disorderly and resend missing parts.

TCP ports. A source port is linked to a destination port by TCP, like from source port 8648 to destination port 67. The port field is 16 bits; port numbers permitted ranges from 0-65,535.

UDP. UDP is faster and simpler than TCP. It is used for applications like audio or video streaming.

ICMP. Internet control message protocol is used to transmit error reports and for troubleshooting. Without the assistance of ICMP, IP would be unable to route ports, networks, or hosts that are down and fix other problems. ICMP uses encryption and types and does not understand ports like UDP and TCP does.

Application-Layer TCP/IP Protocols and Concepts
They are:

Telnet. Telnet provides terminal emulation across a network. "Terminal" is a text-based VT100-style terminal access. Telnet servers listen on TCP port 23. For 20 years, Telnet has been used to access interactive command sell across networks.

It provides no confidentiality, thus is unsafe. Information transferred during a session is in cleartext, in addition to the password and user ID used to log-in to the system.

FTP. File Transfer Protocol (FTP) is used to transfer files. Similar to Telnet, FTP is not secure and has no integrity, thus, isn't used in transmitting sensitive information.

SSH. Secure shell (SSH) was devised as a secure substitute for FTP, the UNIX "R" commands, and Telnet. In addition to other features, it allows integrity, secure log-in, and confidentiality. It can be used to securely channel other protocols, like HTTP.

SMTP, POP, and IMAP. Simple Mail Transfer Protocol (SMTP) is used in sending emails to and from network-servers. It utilizes TCP port 25. Protocols include POPv3 (Post Office Protocol) that uses TCP port 110 and IMAP (Internet Message Access Protocol) that uses TCP port 143.

DNS. Domain Name System (DNS) is a universal database that hierarchically translates IP addresses to names and vice versa. DNS implements TCP and UDP. Small responses implement UDP port 53, whereas bulkier responses, like zone transfers, utilize TCP port 53.

HTTP and HTTPS. HTTP (Hypertext Transfer Protocol) sends unencrypted web-based information while hypertext transfer protocol (HTTPS) sends encrypted web-based information using SSL/TLS. HTTP utilizes TCP port 80, whereas HTTPS utilizes TCP port 443. Web content is shown with HTML (hypertext markup language).

LAN Protocols and Technologies

LAN consists of layers 1–3 technologies like FDDI, ethernet, logical and physical network topologies, network cabling types, and others.

Ethernet. Layer 2 implements ethernet. It is an important local-area networking technology. Here, network information is transmitted using frames. Ethernet uses one channel (baseband), so it fixes problems like collisions, a situation in which two nodes try to send information concurrently.

WAN Protocols and Technologies

ISPs and other network providers, whose networks spread around cities and countries, often make of use WAN technologies.

T1s, T3s, E1s, and E3s. Many international circuit standards exist; the most dominant are T Carriers (United States) and E Carriers (Europe).

Frame Relay. This is a 'packetized' Layer 2 WAN protocol that allows recovery without errors and focuses on speed. When used to convey higher-layer protocols like TCP/IP, authenticity is guaranteed.

MPLS. Multiprotocol label switching presents a way of transmitting WAN information via labels across a shared network. These labels, (not encapsulated header like IP header), makes decisions. MPLS transmits data and voice and is utilized to simplify WAN routing.

Converged Protocols

"Convergence" is a modern network lingo. Ethernet and TCP/IP is used to deliver services like storage, industrial control, and voice, instead of the previously used non-IP networks and devices.

DNP3 (Distributed Network Protocol). This provides a standard required majorly within the energy sector for interoperability across different subscribers' SCADA and smart grid applications. This protocol is multi-layered (unlike most uni-layered protocols like SMTP) and can be transmitted through another multilayer protocol-TCP/IP.

Storage Protocols. Internet Small Computer System Interface (iSCSI) and Fibre Channel over Ethernet (FCoE) are storage area network (SAN) protocols that supply inexpensive ways of authorizing storage interface with protocols and existing network infrastructure technologies. SAN permits block-level file access through a network, like a directly attached hard disk.

FCoE succeeds Fiber Channel, which was previously used for storage networking but does not need completely different cabling and hardware; instead, FCoE is transmitted along standard Ethernet networks. In FCoE, Fiber Channel's host bus adapters (HBAs) can be combined to reduce cost. FCoE uses Ethernet, not TCP/IP. Using TCP/IP, Fibre Channel over IP(FCIP) encapsulates Fiber Channel frames.

Like FCoE, iSCSI is a SAN protocol that allows authorization of storage interface with protocols and existing networking infrastructure. FCoE uses Ethernet, whereas iSCSI makes use of higher-layered TCP/IP for connection. It is routed the same way as any other IP protocol (like FCIP). Because protocols beyond layer 2 (Ethernet) are used, iSCSI can be transmitted across only the local network. iSCSI uses LUNs (Logical Unit Numbers) to solve storage problems across the network. Additionally, LUNs are required for primary access control for network accessible storage.

VoIP. Using data networks, Voice over Internet protocol (VoIP) sends voice; a modification of analog POTS (Plain Old Telephone Service), that is still used after a century. VoIP provides the advantages of packet-switched networks, like reliability and low-cost to the telephone.

Although VoIP provides cheaper options, particularly for new sites without an established legacy voice investment, it is not secured. By default, most VoIP protocols like RTP provide low-level security.

Software-Defined Networks

A router's control plane separates from the data (forwarding) plane by Software-Defined Networking (SDN). The control plane determines routing. Using a router, the data plane sends data (packets). Using SDN routing, decisions are taken remotely rather than on individual routers.

The most common protocol used is OpenFlow, it permits central controller upgrade or assigns control of switching rules. It is a TCP protocol that encrypts using transport layer security (TLS).

Wireless Local-Area Networks (WLANs)

Wireless Local-Area Networks transmits data using light or electromagnetic waves. Radio.802.11 is the most common type of WLAN, 802.11i is the initial variant to guarantee security.

FHSS (Frequency-Hopping Spread Spectrum) and DSSS (Direct-Sequence Spread Spectrum). These are two means of transmitting traffic across the radio.

DSSS makes use of the whole band, "spreading" signals all over the band. A number of small frequency channels are used all over the band by FHSS, and "hops" through them in an order described as pseudorandom.

WEP. The wired equivalent privacy protocol was previously used (authenticated in 1999) to supply 802.11 wireless security. WEP is weak, and WEP passcodes can easily be hacked. It provides little integrity or confidentiality due to these hacks. In reality, many think WEP is unsafe and forbid its use. Rather than WEP, the encryption algorithms indicated in 802.11i or other encryption methods like virtual private networks (VPNs) should be used.

OFDM. Orthogonal Frequency-Division Multiplexing (OFDM) is a recent multiplexing method, which allows simultaneous transmissions to make use of multiple independent wireless frequencies which do not interfere with each other.

802.11i. This is the first 802.11 variant that provides moderate security, a robust security network (RSN), and permits pluggable authentication modules. RSN enables modification of cryptographic ciphers as new weaknesses are discovered.

Bluetooth. According to IEEE standard 802.15, Bluetooth is a PAN wireless technology running on the same 2.4 GHz frequency like few 802.11 devices. Small, low-power gadgets like cell phones use Bluetooth to transmit data along short distances. Version 2.1 and older run on 3 Mbps or less; versions 3 and 4 permits faster speeds.

Sensitive gadgets should block automated detection by Bluetooth devices around. The security of the bluetooth's 48-bit MAC address adapter determines its detection. Bluetooth devices are easily detected (even if disabled) by estimating the MAC address. The primary 24-bits are are easily estimated, they are the OUI, whereas the final 24 bits are estimated aggressively.

Secure Network Devices and Protocols

These devices include:

Repeaters and Hubs

These are Layer 1 devices. Repeaters that obtain information on one port "repeats" on another port. The repeater doesn't comprehend protocols; it only repeats bits. Repeaters could lengthen a network.

A hub is a repeater that has more than two ports, receiving bits on one port and repeating them to other ports.

Bridges

Switches and bridges are Layer 2 devices. Bridges have two collision domains and two ports. They link network sections together. Each section has several nodes. Data transferred from nodes on one end is sent across to the other, while data transferred from the same end of the the bridge is not sent across. The bridge presents traffic separation and makes forwarding decisions by assimilating the MAC addresses of linked nodes.

Switches

These are bridges with over two ports. The best practice is to connect only one device in a switch port. This way, the collision domain is reduced to one port. If each port has just one connected device, no collisions occur. Trunks link multiple switches.

VLANs. A VLAN is a virtual LAN, resembling a virtual switch. Desktops and servers are connected to the same switch to generate different server and desktop LANs. Different switches can be used; alternatively, two separate VLANs can be developed.

One switch can anchor several VLANs, and one VLAN spread across several switches. VLANs may also add defense-in-depth protection to networks by segmenting information and managing traffic.

Routers

These are layer 3 devices that direct traffic between LANs. Source and destination IP addresses determine decisions made by IP-based routers.

Firewalls

Firewalls filter traffic between networks layers 3 and 4 (IP addresses and ports) and determine command followed by stateful firewalls and TCP/IP packet filters. Layers 5–7 determine command followed by proxy firewalls. Firewalls are multihomed - several NICs are linked to several different networks.

Packet filter. This is a simple and fast firewall. A single packet determines every filtering decision. It is impossible to review old packets to make new decisions.

Outgoing ICMP echo commands and incoming ICMP echo responses is permitted by packet filtering firewall. Computer 1 can ping bank.example.com. The problem is: an attacker at evil.example.com can send unrequested echo replies that might be permitted by the firewall.

Stateful firewalls. Stateful firewalls permits the firewall to compare new packets to old ones; though slower than packet filters, they have higher security.

Computer 1 transmits ICMP echo command to bank.example.com. The firewall configures to Internet sites, thus, the stateful firewall permits the data and includes entry to its state table.

Computer 1 then receives an echo reply from bank.example.com. The firewall checks if this traffic is permitted, and transmits the data.

If evil.example.com sends an unrequested ICMP echo response, the stateful firewall detects absent state table entry and the traffic is blocked.

Proxy firewalls. Proxy firewalls function as intermediary servers. Both the packet filter and stateful firewalls allow or block traffic.

Application-Layer Proxy Firewalls. Application-layer proxy firewalls runs up to layer 7. Rather than taking commands on layers 3 and 4 alone (like packet filter and stateful firewalls), application-layer proxies also base decisions on application-layer data like HTTP traffic.

Modem

A modem is a modulator/demodulator that converts binary data to analog sound transmitted on phone networks structured for human voices. Demodulation of the analog sound to binary information is then done by the receiving modem.

Secure Communications

One major problem is safeguarding information in motion. The internet provides inexpensive communication globally with minimal accessibility, security, and integrity.

Authentication Protocols and Frameworks

This certifies and identity claims across a server. Strong security design presumes that packets sent between the client and server can be leaked, therefore, this protocol should be secure.

802-.1X. This is a Port-Based Network Access Control (PNAC) that includes EAP.

EAP. This is a certification model that explains several specific certification protocols. It supplies certification at layer 2 (port-based) prior to a node receiving an IP-address. It is used in wired and wireless but is structured on WLAN. An EAP user is called a supplicant and certification is demanded from an authentication server (AS).

VPN (Virtual Private Networks)

This protects information transmitted on insecure networks like the internet. The objective is to ensure the privacy provided by a circuit like T1. It includes ciphers like AES to guarantee security and cryptographic hashes like SHA-1 to secure authentication

PPP. Point-to-Point Protocol (PPP) is a layer 2 protocol that guarantees security, integrity, and authentication through point-to-point connections. PPP anchors synchronous connections like T1s and asynchronous connections like modems.

IPsec. Security isn't inbuilt on IPv4; higher-layer protocols like TLS provide confidentiality. IPsec (Internet Protocol security) was created to guarantee security, certification, and integrity, through IPv6 encryption, it is ported to IPv4. It is a collection of protocols. The two major types are: Authentication Header (AH) and Encapsulating Security Protocol (ESP). Each is assigned IP protocol number; AH is protocol 51 and ESP is protocol 50.

SSL (Secure Sockets Layer) and TL

SSL safeguards HTTP data. HTTPS utilizes port 443. TLS is a modification of SSL, equal to the SSL version. 3.1.TLS 1.2 is the latest version.

Although initially focused on the web, SSL or TLS can be used in encryption of various kinds of information and channeled through other protocols to create VPN connections. VPNs of SSL are more direct than their IPsec counterparts: IPsec makes changes to IP-networks, thus, installing IPsec software modifies the operating system. SSL client software does not request operating system modifications. Compared to IPsec firewalling SSL is easier.

Remote Access

In this digital age, secured access is crucial. Users are connected through a Digital Subscriber Line (DSL) or cable modem, and recently, remote meeting technology and instant messaging.

Cable Modems. Using broadband cable TV, cable TV suppliers use cable modems to provide internet access. Cable TV access is limited and is available in cities, most large towns, and industries. Contrary to DSL, it is possible to share bandwidth between users using the same platform.

Remote- Desktop Console Access. Two popular modern protocols that allow remote access to a desktop are: Remote Desktop Protocol (RDP) that operates on TCPport3389, and Virtual Network Computing (VNC) that operates on TCP 5900. Contrary to the earlier end-based approach to remote access, they allow graphical access to remote systems.

Desktop and Application Virtualization. This is a technology that supplies a central host for desktop images that are effective remotely. Desktop virtualization, also referred to as VDI, means virtual desktop infrastructure or virtual desktop interface.

Contrary to supplying a full desktop environment, a company can virtualize important applications that are hosted centrally. Linking the central control with application virtualization allows access restriction and patches the application quickly. In addition, application virtualization runs legacy applications which would otherwise be impossible to operate on systems implemented by the workforce.

Screen Scraping. Graphical remote access to systems is facilitated by screen scraping. Screen scraping protocols utilize packet-data and send data used to sketch the accessed system's screen on its display with remote access. A screen scraping approach is the popularly used technology VNC. Although, not every remote access protocol employs screen scraping. For example, RDP does not use employ scraping.

Instant messaging. Instant messaging uses real-time "chat" to allow interaction between two or more users. Chat may involve just two users or many users, like in group chats.

Remote meeting technology. Remote meeting technology is a recent technology that provides a platform for users to hold meetings online on the internet, including desktop sharing. These technologies usually allow PowerPoint slides to display on all PCs linked to a meeting, sharing files like spreadsheets, audio, or video.

Most of these solutions are transmitted across outgoing TSL or SSL traffic, which are sent through web proxies and firewalls. It is necessary to comprehend and manage remote meeting technologies so as to remain up-to-date with every possible policy.

PDA (Personal Digital Assistance). These are small computers that can be placed on the palm. PDAs have been modified, starting with first-generation devices like the Apple Newton and Palm Pilot. These older PDAs provide calendar and note-taking features. PDA operating systems included Windows Mobile, Google's Android, Apple iOS, Windows Mobile, and Blackberry.

Two main problems of PDA security are data loss and wireless security. Sensitive data should be encrypted on PDAs, if not, the device should store only a small amount of information. The device is protected with a PIN and allows a "wipe"- erasing data from the device in case of a theft or loss.

Content distribution networks. Content distribution networks (CDN) use an arrangement of distributed caching servers to enhance performance and decrease the dormancy of downloaded material. They routinely find the servers nearest to users, so content is downloaded from the fastest and closest internet servers. They include: Microsoft Azure, Akamai, CloudFlare, Amazon CloudFront.

Chapter Five

Identity and Access Management

I dentity and access control is the basis for all security disciplines, not only IT security. Access management allows certified users access to relevant data and deny unauthorized users access.

Authentication Methods

The basic principle for employing access control is the valid certification of users. First, a user provides an identification; though, this cannot be trusted. The subject then certifies by supplying an assurance that validates purported identity. A credential set is the combination of the identification and certification of a user.

There are four certification techniques: Type 3 (what you are), Type 2 (what you have), Type 1 (what you know). Someplace you are is the fourth type.

Type 1: What you know

This assesses users with a question and the user must reply correctly. Access is granted based on something they know, like a password or a PIN. This is the easiest; thus the least secure certification type.

Passwords. Three types of passwords are used to execute access management paraphrases, one-time passwords, dynamic passwords, and static passwords.

Static passwords are renewable and may/may not elapse. They are created by the user and are most effective in combination with a different authentication type, like a biometric control or smart card.

Passphrases are long static passwords made up of words in a sentence or phrase. Passphrases can be made stronger by using words that make no sense, thereby allowing room for no guessing (e.g. replacing CISSP with "XYZZY" in the last passphrase), by mixing small letters with capital letters, and by using additional symbols and numbers.[21]

One-time passwords (OTP) are used for a single authentication. They are really secure but difficult to manage. A one-time password can't be renewed and is viable just once.

A dynamic password switches at fixed intervals. RSA security created SecurID, a synchronous device that creates new token codes every minute. The RSA dynamic token code is combined with the user's static password to generate one password that changes each time. A disadvantage is the highly-priced tokens.

Password guessing. Password guessing is an online method that attempts to certify a user into the system. Some web-based hacks use password guessing, so applications should be created with this knowledge. Account lockouts stops a successful password guessing hack.

---

[21] Garfinkel, S., Schwartz, A., & Spafford, G. (2003). *Practical Unix and Internet security*. Beijing: O'Reilly.

Password hashes and password cracking. IT systems do not store clear-text passwords; it only stores the hashed outputs of password. Hashing is a unidirectional encryption utilizing algorithms and no key. Once a user tries to log in, the input password is hashed, and compared with the hash stored on the system. It is impossible to reverse algorithms and generate a password from a hash.; thus, hackers may run the hash algorithm forward several times, thereby choosing several passwords, and comparing the output to a hash, hoping to find a match (thus getting the original password). This is known as password cracking.

Dictionary attacks. A dictionary hacks utilizes word lists, and all are hashed. If the hacking software corresponds to hash output obtained from a dictionary hack, the original password is obtained.

Hybrid attacks. A hybrid attack supplements or modifies characters in the words from a dictionary prior to hashing, this allows cracking of complicated passwords quickly. For example, a hacker may have a list of possible passwords but will also replace letter "o" with number "0".

Brute-force attacks. Brute-force attacks are time-consuming but are more effective. The attacker estimates the hash outputs for all probable passwords. Years ago, computer speed was very slow and made this difficult. Advancements in CPU speeds and parallel computing has made brute-force attacks on complicated passwords faster.

Rainbow tables. A rainbow table represents a database containing the already-hashed output for all probable passwords. Its generation is slow and is always incomplete; sometimes all possible password/hash combinations may not be included. Although, rainbow tables represents a database, they are complicated, using a memory/time switch to represent and retrieve passwords.

Salts. Salts allow one password to hash severally. Most systems incorporates salt with password prior to hashing. Although storing hashes is much superior to storing plaintext passwords, with a salt value, the same password will encrypt in a different manner different users make use of it.

Type 2: Something you have

This certification demands that a client possesses an item like a token that confirms a user's identity

Synchronous dynamic tokens. They utilize counters or time to align a presented token code with a code required by the authentication server. Those that utilize time displays token codes that change at intervals, like each minute; the code is viable only during that session.

Asynchronous dynamic tokens. They are never synchronized with a central server. Challenge-response tokens are the most popular type.

Type 3: Something you are

In the Type 3 authentication (something you are), physical properties certify or identify users using biometrics. For example: an airport facial recognition or a fingerprint scanner.

Biometric enrollment and throughput. Enrollment is the process of registering using a biometric system; this means creating a new account. A username and a password/PIN is provided, then biometric data, like placing fingerprints on a fingerprint reader or taking a photograph of the iris. Enrollment is done only once, lasting for less than 2 minutes.

Throughput (or biometric response time) is the certification process in a biometric system; this lasts for 6–10 seconds.

Accuracy of biometric systems. Prior to executing a biometric control program; the accuracy should be reviewed. Three metrics can be used in evaluating biometric prevision:

- **False reject rate.** This happens when a certified user is not accepted (uncertified) by the biometric system. This is also called Type I error.

- **False accept rate.** This is when an uncertified user is certified. If several false rejections are generated by the biometric control of a company, the overall control has to adjust the system's accuracy by reducing the quantity of information received during user certification. Reduction of information increases the risk of false acceptance; thus, risks allowing access to an uncertified user. This is a Type II error.

- **Crossover error rate.** The CER (or Equal Error Rate - EER) is the point at which FRR and FAR become equivalent. It describes a biometric system's entire accuracy.   Increasing sensitivity of a biometric system increases FRRs and reduces FARs and vice versa.

Types of biometric controls

Today, several biometric controls are utilized, including:

- Fingerprints

- Retina scan

- Iris scan

- Hand geometry

- Keyboard dynamics.

- Dynamic signature

- Voiceprint

- Facial scan

Someplace you are

Someplace you are, is a location-based access management that utilizes technologies like the IP address-based geolocation, the physical location for a purchase or global positioning system (GPS). If the user is in the wrong location, access is blocked.

Access Control Technologies

Centralized Access Control. It allows one-point access management for an organization. Rather than making use local access control databases, certification is through third-party access controls. It also provides single sign-on, where the user may certify once, and several systems are accessed. Centralized access management makes the three As of access control available. They include

- [22] Authentication: confirming an identity claim.

- Authorization: certified users can operate a system.

- Accountability: the capability to analyze a system and show the users' actions.

Decentralized Access Control. This allows the administration of IT to happen close to the system's mission and operations. Here, an organization spreads across multiple locations, while every local site maintain and support independent systems, data, and access control databases.

This ensures greater local power because every site controls its data. Although it is empowering, it has its own risks. Various websites may implement different policies, level of security, and access management models, this results in discrepancies. Companies that have a general policy may discover that adherence is different on every website. The weakest chain is the most vulnerable to hacks. For example, a small company with few trained staff is a better target than a data controlling center that has highly-trained employees.

Single Sign-On. This enables several systems to utilize a central AS, permits one-time certification and access to several systems. It also enables security administrators to append, change, or deny user privileges on a central system. Its major disadvantage is that it may grant a hacker access to information once one certification technique,

---

[22] Fundamentals of Information Systems Security/Access Control Systems - Wikibooks, open books for an open world. (2019). Retrieved from https://en.wikibooks.org/wiki/Fundamentals_of_Information_Systems_Security/Access_Control_Systems

like a password, is breached. Due to this, SSO should always be utilized with multifactor certification.

Access Review, Audit, and User Entitlement. Access aggregation is when one user is granted access to several systems. This can be deliberate, like in SSO, or accidentally, as users can be granted new access rights once they begin new duties. This produces authorization creep, where users gain additional access without relinquishing old ones. These access rights can be compounded over time. User Access must be reviewed and analyzed regularly. Improvements should be made to block previous access once new access is granted.

Federated Identity Management. Federated identity management (FIdM) or identity management (IdM) utilizes SSO at a wider range; from cross-organization to Internet scale.

As defined by EDUCAUSE, "Identity management describes the technologies, policies, and procedures that confirm user identities and implement regulations about access to digital content." On a campus, many data systems—like the library database, email, grid computing applications, and learning management systems requests user certification (username and password). A certification process determines which systems and which certified user is granted access. In an enterprise identity management system, instead of using different credentials for each system, a user utilizes one digital identity to access all resources to which the user is qualified. FIdM extends this approach beyond the enterprise level, generating a secured authorization for digital identities. In a federated system, organizations involved share identity characteristics based on previously approved standards, improving certification from other associates of the federation and

91

allowing access to contents online. This method simplifies access to digital resources while securing limited contents.

SAML. FIdM utilizes SAML (Security Association Markup Language) or OpenID. SAML is XML-based and exchanges security data. Extensible Markup Language (XML) is a markup language that provides a standardized way of encrypting information and files. SAML promotes web SSO on an internet scale.

Identity as a Service. Identity is a prerequisite to manage integrity, security, and accessibility successfully. Cloud identity or identity as a service (IDaaS) allows organizations to replace cloud service. Like all security matters, components of cloud identity increases or decreases.

Microsoft accounts are an example of cloud identity commonly used in organizations.

LDAP (Lightweight Directory Access Protocol). This supplies an open protocol that interfaces and questions directory service data provided by network operating systems. LDAP is commonly used for large identity services which include Active Directory. Directory services play a crucial role in many applications by revealing key user, computer, services, and other objects to be queried through LDAP.

LDAP is the application layer protocol which uses port 389 through TCP user datagram protocol (UDP). LDAP queries can be sent in clear text and are determined by configuration and enables anonymous query of all/some information. LDAP back certified connections and secures communication channels leveraging TLS.

Access Control Protocols and Frameworks. Centralized and decentralized models enable remote user certification in local systems.

Protocols used to support this requirement include RADIUS, Diameter, TACACS/TACACS+, PAP, and CHAP.

RADIUS. RADIUS (Remote Authentication Dial-in User Service) protocol is a third-party certification. it utilizes UDP ports 1813(accounting) and 1812 (certification). It previously employed the unofficial ports of 1646 and 1645 respectively.

RADIUS confirms a user's certifications against a certification database. It certifies users by granting particular users access to particular data. It records every window session by generating a log entry for every RADIUS connection.

Diameter. Diameter succeeds RADIUS and has a better AAA system. RADIUS restricts accountability, confidentiality, and integrity; these properties are improved in Diameter.

TACACS (Terminal Access Controller Access Control System) and TACACS+. The TACACS requests user ID and static password for verification. It makes use of the UDP port 49 as well as TCP. Though, reusable passwords result in less security; the improved TACACS+ protects passwords with a stronger certification.

TACACS+ uses TCP port 49. PAP (Password Authentication Protocol) isn't confidential: the input password is transmitted through the network in cleartext. It is then received and certified by PAP server. Network-sniffing may expose the cleartext passwords.

Access Control Models

The different access control models include the following;

Discretionary Access Controls

DAC allows users to totally control objects that have been granted access to, and also share the objects with other users where they can also modify or delete files. Users can manage their own data. Windows OS and Standard UNIX use DAC.

Mandatory Access Controls

This is a system-enforced access management model that is determined by a user's clearance and an object's labels, like confidential, secret, and top-secret. An object is accessed by a user only if the user's clearance is the same as or higher than the object's label. Users can't share objects with other users with an invalid clearance, to a lower classification level (like from secret to confidential). MAC systems is primarily based on retaining information confidentiality.

Non-Discretionary Access Control

Role-Based Access Control (RBAC) explains data access depending on the function of the user. Functions could be a nurse, a backup administrator, or a help desk technician. Function, not user, determines access.

RBAC is a non-discretionary access management model as users do not know the category of the object they are allowed to access and cannot send objects to other users.

Another non-discretionary access control model is task-based access management, elated to RBAC. It is determined by the activities performed by each user, like writing prescriptions or retrieving or revealing a help desk ticket. It tries to fix the same problem as RBAC but focuses on predefined activities instead of functions.

Rule-Based Access Controls

A rule-based access management model utilizes a set of guidelines, filters, and limitations for accessing objects in a system.

Content-Dependent and Context-Dependent Access Controls

Content-dependent and context-dependent access controls are not entirely considered access management techniques like DAC and MAC; they only support defense-in-depth. They are included as supplementary control in DAC systems.

Content-dependent access control provides additional criteria than certification and identification.

Chapter Six

Security Assessment and Testing

Security assessment and testing are important components of any data security program. Organizations must thoroughly evaluate their real-world security, focusing on the most important components to make relevant modifications.

Two main elements of assessment are software testing using static and dynamic passwords and overall security assessment (penetration testing, vulnerability scanning, and security analysis).

Assessing Access Control

Many tests help to evaluate the success of access control. Tests with a narrow range include security audits, penetration tests, and vulnerability assessment.

Penetration Testing

A penetration tester is a white-hat attacker who gets certified to try to hack an organization's physical or electronic perimeter (or both). Penetration tests ("pen tests") determines if black hat hackers could do the same. Though narrow; they are beneficial, particularly with an efficient penetration tester.[23]

Penetration tests are:

- Network (Internet)
- Network (DMZ or internal)
- Wireless
- War dialing
- Physical (attempt to gain entrance into a facility or room)

Hacks include user hacks, server attacks, or application attacks.

Partial-knowledge tests are intermediate between complete and zero knowledge; the penetration tester gets restricted internal information.

Penetration testers frequently use penetration testing tools, which include the open-source Metasploit, closed-source Core Impact, and Immunity Canvas. Pen testers also use customized tools, malware samples, and encryptions posted on the web.

Penetration testers utilize these techniques:

- Planning
- Reconnaissance
- Enumeration (or scanning)
- Vulnerability assessment
- Exploitation
- Reporting

Black hat hackers use similar techniques although less planning is done and reporting is omitted; they also cover their bases by erasing log

---

[23] CISSP – Adventures in the programming jungle. (2019). Retrieved from https://adriancitu.com/category/certification/cissp/page/2/

entry and other signs of invasion, sometimes they bypass system integrity by installing back-doors to allow access. A penetration tester must always safeguard information and guarantee integrity.

Prior to starting the penetration test, signs of old or new successful hacks might be seen. Sometimes, penetration testers discover that a system has been breached previously. Hackers are more malicious once discovered, compromising system and user integrity. If system integrity of the system is compromised, a penetration test should be stopped and escalated.

Finally, the concluding penetration test report must have high-level security, because its content can be used to breach the system.

Vulnerability Testing

Vulnerability scanning (or testing) scans a network or system for a list of predefined weaknesses like system misconfiguration, expired software, and an absence of patching. Vulnerability-testing tools include Nessus and OpenVAS.

Security Audits

A security audit assesses by comparing to a recognized standard. For example, companies are analyzed for Payment Card Industry Data Security Standard (PCI DSS) compliance. PCI DSS involves several compulsory controls, like specific access to management programs, wireless encoding, and firewalls. An auditor then verifies if a site or company meets the recognized standard.

Security Assessments

This is a comprehensive approach to evaluating the competence of access management. There are broader scopes of security assessments that extends beyond penetration tests or vulnerability scanning

The objective of including specific tests like a penetration test is to ascertain that every aspect of access control is included.

Log Reviews

Assessing security audit entries in an IT system is an easy ways to check the performance of access management models.

The information obtained from the audit log entries and can be helpful; the current state of malware in thousands of systems can be accurately known from the obtained antivirus entries from these systems. Antivirus alerts alongside spikes in unsuccessful certification alerts from servers, or an increase in outgoing firewall barricades confirms that password-guesses is trying to access a network.

Software Testing Techniques

There are different software testing methods. As an addition to testing the software stability and characteristics, testing also detects specific programmer errors which leads to a breach in system integrity and lack bound checking. The two techniques of assessing encryptions automatically are:

Static and Dynamic Testing

Static testing assesses encryptions passively (when the code is not running) This includes syntax checking, code assessments, and walkthroughs. Static analysis tools assesses the original encryption source code while checking for functions, insecure practices, libraries, and other features used in the source encryptions.

Dynamic testing assesses the code or application while executing it.

Both methods are adequate and are complementary. Static analysis tools may find irregularities in encryptions that have not been completely implemented in a manner that reveals the irregularity to dynamic testing. However, dynamic analysis may find lags in a particular code execution missed by the static analysis.

White-box software assessment grants the user access to encryption source, variables, and data structures. Black-box testing gives the user no internal information; the software is like a black-box that obtains data.

Traceability Matrix

A traceability matrix, or a Requirements Traceability Matrix (RTM), is used to map user requirements to the software assessment plan. It traces these requirements and ensures their fulfillment by linking client usage to test examples.

Synthetic Transactions

Synthetic transactions (monitoring) include creating tools or commands or tools that simulate activities implemented in an application. The objective of using synthetic monitoring is to standardize transaction strength. These transactions can be programmed to operate at intervals to confirm the application is still running as it should be. They can also be used in assessing program updates before distribution to ensure that functionality and performance will not be affected adversely. This type of monitoring is commonly utilized in custom-developed web programs.

Software Testing Levels

Employing various software testing methods is important, assessing various testing levels from low to high.

Fuzzing

Fuzz testing is a variant of black-box testing that transmits random, malformed information as inputs into software programs to check if it crashes. If a program crashes after transmitting/obtaining unrequested data, there might be a boundary-checking problem and it might be vulnerable to a buffer overflow hack. If a program crashes or hangs, it has failed the fuzz test.[24]

Combinatorial Software Testing

This is a black-box assessment technique that attempts to identify and assess every possible combination of inputs.

Misuse Case Testing

Misuse case assessment uses cases for programs, which determines how different functionalities are ranked in an application. Formal use cases are constructed as a flow diagram written by Unified Modeling Language(UML) and are structured to model standard functions and commands.

Misuse case testing shows how a security impact could be detected by copying the replication the possible actions of the enemy on the system. This could be seen as a variant of 'use case' but the purpose of

---

[24] Syed Ubaid Ali jafri - CISSP Exam Guide by Eric Conrad,Seth Misenar. (2019). Retrieved from http://docslide.us/education/syed-ubaid-ali-jafri-cissp-exam-guide-by-eric-conradseth-misenar.html

misuse case assessment is to detect the complete lack of hacks on the programs.

Test Coverage Analysis

This seeks to identify the scope of code testing in the whole application. Its objective is to ensure that no gaps, which in the absence of testing could permit bugs or security problems, are present.

Interface Testing

Interface testing is majorly focused on exposing adequate functionality, extending across all the ways users can interact with the application. The objective is to ensure that security is evenly applied throughout all the interfaces. This kind of testing assesses the various attack vectors that could be leveraged by a hacker.

Chapter Seven

Security Operations

‗‗‗

S ecurity operations is concerned with threats to a production environment. Threat agents are either internal or external. Security operations include hardware, media, people, and data, together with associated threats of each.

Administrative Security

Every company consists of data, people, and a method for people to utilize data. Operations security ensures that people are restricted from deliberately or accidentally breaching the confidentiality, integrity, or accessibility of information/systems and data storage media.

Administrative Personnel Controls

Administrative personnel controls are vital elements of operations security that must be understood by a CISSP candidate. These are elements within information security that are transmitted through various domains.[25]

---

[25] Syed Ubaid Ali jafri - CISSP Exam Guide by Eric Conrad,Seth Misenar. (2019). Retrieved from http://docslide.us/education/syed-ubaid-ali-jafri-cissp-exam-guide-by-eric-conradseth-misenar.html

Least Privilege or Minimum Necessary Access. The principle of least privilege is a very important concepts of information security, also called the principle of minimum necessary access. It states that 'people should be granted access strictly needed for performing their functions, not more.' Following this principle is a basic security dogma and functions as the starting point for administrative controls.

Need to Know. For companies that deal with highly sensitive data that uses mandatory access control (MAC), a vital determination of access is implemented by the system in companies with very sensitive information, determined by the user's clearance levels and object's classification levels. Though the screening process for someone accessing very sensitive material is strict, clearance level alone is not adequate when handling sensitive data. The concept of compartmentalization is an expansion of the principle of least privilege in MAC environments.

Compartmentalization, allows implementation of need to know, extending beyond only clearance level and requires simply that someone must be granted access to data. Consider a very sensitive military operation; although there may be a large number of people, some might rank higher, only a few will "need to know" relevant information. Other people don't "need to know," thus are denied access.

Separation of Duties. This requires that several individuals are needed to finalize sensitive or important transactions. The objective is to ensure that an individual does not misuse access to sensitive information as misuse happens jointly. Collusion is when the two individuals collide to abuse information security.

Rotation of Duties. Rotation of duties, also known as responsibilities or job rotation, creates a way for a company to reduce the risk connected with someone having unfettered access. Job rotation entails that an individual performs important duty for limited period. Different problems can be solved by job rotation; This can be illustrated by an "hit by a bus" scenario. Picture an individual in the company is hit by a truck. If the outcome of the death of an individual might be enormous, then perhaps one way to lessen this impact would be to make sure that there is additional coverage for this individual's responsibilities in the event of his/her absence or demise.

Compulsory Leave or Vacation. Compulsory leave (forced vacation) is another organizational activity that is very similar to duty rotation. Although there are valid reasons for granting employees leave of absence or time away from official duties, the main considerations include:

1. To reduce or prevent stress-induced errors.

2. To detect employees weak points while away.

3. To detect and prevent fraud.

All of these are similar to the reasons for duty rotation.

Pre-employment screening (Background checks). A number of organizations that carry out background checks (pre-employment screening) as an administrative control measures before employment. Each organization will decide how deep they are willing to dig into a potential employee's record. Some might carry out hasty, superficial background checks such as the criminal record of such individuals while others may go further to confirm previous work history, credentials and qualifications, and may even request for drug screening test results.

A Non-Disclosure agreement (NDA). Before an employee or corporate body is granted access to highly sensitive confidential information, they- must sign an NDA form. What is an NDA? This is a contractual agreement that will ensure that the confidentiality of information, while an employee has access to it, will be maintained and never disclosed to others not involved the agreement. It places a legal responsibility upon those involved to maintain the confidentiality of such sensitive information. Those who usually are involved in this kind of agreements are job seekers before being employed, external consultants, auditors, contractors, corporate organizations, board members, etc.

Most often than not, NDAs are signed based on directives from above.

Forensics

Just as we have crime forensics which help to gather information at crime scenes so also we have digital forensics. The main aim of forensics is to avoid unintentional modification of the system. This is to offer a strategic approach for investigations and intelligence to gather evidence while giving careful consideration also to the legal implications involved in this process. This can include the preservation of evidence at the scene of the crime in order not to alter the integrity of both the data and the environment of the data unintentionally, for this will be considered a violation of the evidence.

A live forensic involves gathering data and intelligence about the running processes of a system, taking bits of the binary images for physical memory, and gathering data for network connection.

Forensics Media Analysis

Apart from the vital data captured during the live forensic process, the primary source of forensic data is usually binary images of smaller storage devices also known as secondary storage devices. For example: DVDs, USB flash drives, hard disk drives (HDD), CDs, and in some cases connected handsets or portable music players (such as mp3 players).[26]

Network Forensics (NF)

Network Forensics (NF) is similar to network intrusion detection; the main difference is that network intrusion deals with legalities, but network forensics deals with operations. What then is network forensics? NF is a strategic attempt aimed at studying data in motion while cautiously specially focusing on the process of gathering evidence that could be useful in a law court as evidence. Therefore, the integrity of the data must not be compromised or tampered with either intentionally or unintentionally during the forensic process.

Embedded Device Forensics

For decades, forensic investigators had invested so much time, energy, and financial resources to acquire knowledge and invent tools and methods that can analyze devices such as the magnetic disks. However, new technologies such as high-tech, electronic hardware as well as other ED poses a major challenge to investigators in the field of digital forensics. There are no forensic tools to investigate devices like the solid-state drives which are beyond the comprehension of forensic experts.

---

[26] What is Secondary Memory? - Definition from Techopedia. (2019). Retrieved from https://www.techopedia.com/definition/2280/secondary-memory

Electronic Discovery (e-DISCOVERY)

e-Discovery grants legal counsel access to sensitive electronic information gathered during a forensic investigation as one of the pretrial proceedings of a legal case. This will enable the legal counsel to gather sufficient evidence needed to build a case. This is different from regular discovery because e-Discovery deals with electronically stored information (ESI) that has been gathered during forensic investigation. e-Discovery could be both logistically and financially tasking considering the large amount of electronic data which organizations might have in store. Another challenge of e-discovery results from the type of policy adopted by such organization.

In order to reduce or completely avoid the logistic and financial burden of e-discovery, every organization needs to develop certain data storage policies, as well as software designed to enhance the recovery of ESI for e-discovery. When deliberating on which data retention policies to adopt, ensure that such policies will grant:

1. Long term storage of information.

2. Long term access to stored information.

3. Easy deletion of data which are no longer needed.

Incident Response Management

There is a high possibility that every organization will face a major security challenge at one point or another. Holding onto this fact, due to certainty of security incidents eventually impacting organizations, it is therefore imperative that each organization prepare ahead to facilitate prompt detection and response. A well tested, reliable, and recommended method should therefore be adopted.

Methodologies

Various terminologies are used by different writers to describe the process of incident response; however, this section will focus on three easy terms which are: containment, eradication (mitigation), and recovery.

There are eight steps involved in response management:

Preparation. This refers to the precautionary measure employed before the occurrence of an incident. Such measures includes: staff training, listing and pasting a standard incident response procedures at strategic positions, and purchasing computers with software application that could detect malware, etc. Part of a preparation procedure should include a stepwise line of action to be taken when there is an incident. This should be carefully recorded in an incident handbook because in the face of a crisis, there will be lots of confusion, tension, and stress.

Detection/Identification. Detection is one of the key steps involved in incident response management. This step involves the identification or analysis of a series of events so as to determine whether such events have the potential to compromise the security of stored data or cause an ugly incident. If the in-built information system of an organization has detection potential or capacity, such an organization is prone to security incidents and a response might be ineffective or too late.

Response/Containment. At this stage, there is an incident that needs an urgent response and the response team troubleshoots in an attempt to arrest the incident as well as contain or limit the extent of damage caused by the incident. Containment might require that a system is taken offline till the incident is arrested, require the isolation of traffic, or switching off the system completely, etc. But generally, the extent of damage caused by the incident will determine the response. It is at this level that a forensic backup of the affected systems takes place, especially for volatile data.

Mitigation/Eradication. At this stage, the incident team attempts to understand the source of the incidence in a bid to wipe out the threat and restore the system to full operation during the recovery stage. Without detecting the source of an incidence, it will be difficult if not impossible for an organization to rise above an incident, else, there could be a case of reoccurrence or persistence which is too much risk to take. The system should only be restored to full operation only when concrete evidence is available that the threat has been removed. One common mistake most organizations make is to eliminate the most visible threats such as a malfunctioning malware meanwhile that might not be the cause but rather a symptom of a more destructive but insidious malware.

After arresting the threat, the system still needs additional work in order to resume full operational function. This could require restoring the information that was backed up on another reliable backup or rebuilding the system all over again depending on the extent of the damage.

Reporting. This process cuts across all the other stages of incident management starting from detection. Once a malicious function is suspected, reporting must commence immediately. There are two areas of reporting, these are nontechnical and technical reporting. The teams involved in incident management give a detailed technical report of the incident once they commence their activities and should report to management as soon as any serious threat is detected. While trying to address the incident as soon as possible, most teams make the mistake of not reporting back to the management and focus only on the technical aspects. Other nontechnical individuals such as shareholders, investors, owners, etc., should be informed as soon as possible and should be given an update on the latest developments.

Recovery. At this stage, the system is restored to full operational function. Traditionally, a unit that is responsible for the use and care of the system will determine when the system will be set to go online. Keep in mind that it is possible for the other threat to survive the eradication stage. Therefore, it is imperative that the system is closely monitored even after the system is back online.

Remediation. Both remediation and mitigation go hand-in-hand. Remediation involves addressing the cause of the incident while mitigation involves reducing the extent of damage caused by an incident. Thus, even after mitigation, remediation continues. For instance, if the report from the incident team shows that a stolen password was used to cause harm to the system, the mitigation solution might be to change the password and the system will be back online. But the long term remediation procedure might include establishing a two-factor authentication security system for all systems that can be used to access highly sensitive information.

Lessons Learned/Post-Incident Reporting. This stage is meant to give a conclusive report to the management about the cause of the incident, how it was handled and further measures that have been put in place to prevent future occurrence. Also, the report should suggest better ways in which threats could be detected much sooner, ways to enhance prompt responses in the future, and further areas that need improvements. These include possible faults of the organization that led to the incident, and what other elements might have room for improvement. The report from this phase will serve as the basis for future preparation and the lesson learned will be helpful when faced with similar incidents in the future

Root-Cause Analysis.

It is imperative that the affected organization identify the weak points within their system which the enemy was able to exploit in order to effectively prevent or handle future occurrence. Without detecting this, there could be further attack or a recurrence in the future. Also, the system could be launched with an already compromised system which would be disastrous.

Operational Controls: Prevention and Detection

Let us now discuss various devices that could be used to detect and control threats which are necessary for every organization. Some are quite expensive such as antivirus, while others like switches and routers are less expensive.

Intrusion Detection System (IDS) and Intrusion Prevention System (IPS)

IDS can detect and identify any malicious interference, such as policy violation, while IPS is designed to prevent intrusions. The two types include:

- Network-based.

- Host-based.

Types of IDS and IPS Events

We have 4 types of IDS events, and we will illustrate these events using two commonly used streams:

- **True positive:** When a worm spreads across a secured network; NIDS will flag a signal.

- **True negative:** When someone visits an unrestricted site; NIDS gives no danger signal.

- **False positive:** Occurs when a user visits an unrestricted site, yet NIDS flags a signal

- **False negative:** When a worm is spread across a secured network; but NIDS gives no warning signal

It is most desirable to have just true positives and negatives results. However, most IDS will also detect both false negative and false positive results as well. When there are false positives signals, it is seen as a threat and at the end, valuable time and resources are wasted.

Even at that, there is nothing more disastrous than a false negative event because malicious traffic could easily spread unhindered without detection.

NIDS and NIPS. NIDS are devices that detects only suspicious traffic that is found on a network without disrupting the traffic it was designed to monitor. They could scan the security base or firewall of the network (read-only mode) and then forward the alerts to the NIDS Management through another (such as a read/write) interface network.

Unlike NIDS, NIPS obstruct network transmission once malicious traffic is detected.

Types of NIPS include

- Active response.

- Inline response.

The main difference between both is the manner of response. For instance, an active response of NIPS can use TCP RST or send ICMP to port or host destination and eventually shoot down such malicious traffic.

On the other hand, an inline NIPS, as the name implies, acts like a layer made up of about 3–7 firewalls that might either allow or prevent traffic.

Generally, NIPS provides a supportive in-depth defense to complement the role of a firewall; it should therefore be considered a complement to firewalls and not as a replacement. Keep in mind that a false positive alert from a NIP will cause more damage compared to a false positive from a NIDS; this is because even legitimate traffic will be hindered along with the malicious ones which will ultimately affect productivity.

NIPS and NIDS have separate roles and one should not be considered as a replacement for another. Also, each one is established on different rules, for example NIDS has a set of complex rules while NIPS is made up of fewer set of rules, thus; most networks utilize both NIPS and NIDS.

Host-Based Intrusion Prevention Systems (HIPS) And Host-Based Intrusion Detection Systems (HIDS). HIPS and HIDS like NIDS and

NIPS are also host-based. Both can process data and network traffic within the host as it enters the host.

Security Information And Event Management (SIEM)

The main function of SIEM is to ensure and correlate the highly confidential data. When data is correlated, it makes it easier to understand and detect the various risks the organization is exposed to on various security frameworks. Generally, SIEMs have in-built alerts system that can detect specific correlated information, yet it can be modified to follow certain correlation rules to compliment the in-built capacity.

Prevention of Data Loss

Despite the amount of effort and resources directed towards the fight against security breaches, this precarious act continues to abound unabated. Among the brilliant efforts designed to counter this menace is Data Loss Prevention (DLP). DLP refers to a group of security packages that are specially designed to detect and/or prevent the transfer of data from an organization without proper authorization.

Endpoint Security

Most attackers target the endpoints because endpoints provide extra layers that are not under the protection of the network security devices. But in recent times, the new types of endpoints are designed with more sophisticated security countermeasures rather than the common antivirus software.

Another extra feature of these modern endpoint suites is that they are able to detect and prevent encrypted communications as well, even if the encryption was designed to attack that particular endpoint

Antivirus Softwares. Antivirus software is just a layer of a sophisticated endpoint security system. Most antivirus software are programmed to detect malware based on certain signatures detected.

Application Whitelisting. A new invention that has been added to endpoint security suites is application whitelisting. Just as the name implies, a set of binaries is served to the security system which forms the baseline, and binaries not on the whitelist will not be executed. The only loophole is that once a well-known or familiar binary is stolen, it can be manipulated and used to attack the system, creating a security breach.

Detachable Media Controls. Mobile detachable devices can be used as a weapon in attacking and breaching the security system of an organization. There are two ways of executing this plan.

1. Removable media already infected with malware can be attached to the computers of a well-protected organization so as to compromise the organization's security.

2. Secondly, a large volume of data can be stored on very small detachable devices and maliciously used to extract highly sensitive information from the database.

Encrypted Disks. Disk encryption referred to as full disk encryption software is one of the most reliable endpoint security product that is commonly employed.

As seen in partial disk encryption, there is the risk of storing highly sensitive information on an unencrypted portion of the disk.

Asset Management

To provide complete security of operational data, organizations must concentrate on every aspect that could cause a breach such as: The systems, people/staffs, data, and media.

The overall system's security is a key component that guarantees full operational security control and therefore should be given special attention in order to system security protect and prolong the lifespan of the entire system.

Configuration Management

Configuration management involves activities such as:

- Disabling non-essential services.

- Deactivating extraneous programs.

- Installing and activating of security systems like firewalls, antivirus, and intrusion detection, etc.

Baselining. The present security baseline that is in use by an organization can be captured for future use in case of an attack or security incident in the future. It makes it easier for the incident team to respond promptly and more effectively.

Vulnerability Management. Vulnerability checks are carried out to test the security system's strength as well as the vulnerability of stored information. Both remediation and/or mitigation should be effected immediately based on the vulnerability level detected.

Continuity of Operations

Service Level Agreements (SLA)

(SLA) are utilized by service providing organizations or departments to dictate the pros and cons, what is generally acceptable service delivery time, bandwidth, etc.

Fault Tolerance

Making provisions for fault tolerance is very important if service delivery units or organizations are to meet up with operational demands. That way, there will always be availability of services when due.

Redundant Array of Inexpensive Disks (RAID). RAID is designed to reduce the risk related to hard disk failure. Even when one backup disk is used to store data for the recovery of a system, it might take a very long time to fully restore all the data thus, the need for RAID.[27]

We have different RAID levels each with its unique configuration:

- RAID- 0: STRIPED SET: This utilizes striping configuration which enhances the overall activities of read and write data. However, striping prevents data redundancy, thus, RAID 0 isn't recommended for the recovery of highly sensitive data.

- RAID- 1: MIRRORED SET: This can duplicate (copy) or write all data on a disk exactly as they are.

---

[27] RAID level 0, 1, 5, 6 and 10 | Advantage, disadvantage, use. (2019). Retrieved from https://www.prepressure.com/library/technology/raid

- RAID- 2: HAMMING CODE: This is prohibitively expensive because it needs about 39 or 14 hard disks as well as a special hardware controller to function.

- RAID- 3: STRIPED SET WITH DEDICATED PARITY: This also makes use of striping configuration at the level of byte to enhance performance required for transferring data to multiple disks. So as to overcome the challenge of redundancy observed in RAID 0, an extra disk is used in storing parity information in case recovery failure occurs.

- RAID- 4: STRIPED SET WITH DEDICATED PARITY (BLOCK LEVEL): This is very similar to RAID 3 except that data stripping occurs at the block level as opposed to the byte level noticed in RAID 3. Also, RAID 4 utilizes a special parity drive.

- RAID- 5: STRIPED SET WITH DISTRIBUTED PARITY: RAID 5 is among the most commonly used RAID configurations. Unlike RAIDs 3 & 4, RAID 5 distributes the parity information across multiple disks rather than a dedicated disk.

The advantages of RAID 5 include:

  o Lower disk cost for redundancy compared to the cost of a mirrored set.

  o It also has a better time gaining performance improvements associated with RAID 0.

- o RAID 5 allows for data recovery in case one of the disks fails (just one disk will not affect its performance).

- RAID- 6: STRIPED SET WITH DUAL-DISTRIBUTED PARITY: Unlike RAID 5 which can only perform with a single disk failure, RAID 6 still performs well despite the failure of 2 disk drives. This is because redundancy is copied of the same parity information is copied on two separate disks.

- RAID 1 + 0 or RAID 10: This is a good example of a multi-RAID. It is the combination of two different RAID level functionings as one. The configuration of RAID 10 (or RAID 1+0) shows the nesting of a striped set of mirrors.

System Redundancy

Redundant- Hardware and Redundant systems. Internal hardware is found in components prone to damage or failure. A good example of a component with in-built redundancy systems (alternative system) is the power unit in case of power supply failure.

High- Availability Clusters (Failover Cluster). This utilizes multiple interconnected system, in case one system to fails, the other will carry on ensuring continued availability of services.

Load balancing occurs across each unit i.e each system of the active-active HA cluster actively processes data before a system failure occurs. This configuration is however much more expensive than having an active-passive or a standby configuration, in which case backup systems will be activated only when the system fails.

Business Continuity Planning (BCP) And Disaster Recovery Planning (DRP) - Overview And Process

There are a lot of misconceptions about the meaning of BCP and DRP. However both terms are important for CISSP candidates, therefore, there is a need to shed more light on both terms.[28]

BCP

Although both terms are used interchangeably by some organizations, they are however different concepts. It is true that both important to effectively and successfully manage unexpected occurrences, yet they differ in their meaning. BCP ensure the smooth running of the business before, during, and after an unforeseen occurrence. BCP focuses on the entire business, and ensures that business activities will continue with or without a disaster.

DRP

Unlike BBCP, DRP is provided to serve for a short period i.e. during an IT-related interruption such as preventing the spread of a virus (malware) infection across the entire system. One thing you need to know about DRP is that it addresses a particular IT disruption. DRP is therefore considered to be strategic rather than tactical, thus providing a way out of an ugly incident.

Association Between BCP And DRP

BCP can be considered as a universal set with lots of inter-related subsets that addresses a particular problem - a good example is DRP.

---

[28] Jorrigala, Vyshnavi, "Business Continuity and Disaster Recovery Plan for Information Security" (2017). Culminating Projects in Information Assurance. 44. http://repository.stcloudstate.edu/msia_etds/44

Disruptive Events

It is necessary that organizations foresee and then plan ahead for likely disruptive events. Below is a table giving examples of possible events:

Disruptive events	Type
Tsunami, tornado, flood, etc.	Natural
Equipment failure	Environmental
Cyber attack	Human - intentional or technical
Service interruption	Human - intentional or technical
Errors and omissions	Human - unintentional
Electrical fire	Environmental

Process Involved in Disaster Recovery

After differentiating between DRP and BCP, let us now discuss the basic steps leading to recovery after a disaster.

Response. The first step to disaster recovery process is to estimate the extent of the disaster. It helps the disaster management team know if the incident can really be termed a disaster. However, this must be done as soon as possible to help mitigate damage.

Activate Team. Once the incident has been confirmed to be a disaster, the next step is to activate a recovery immediately. The extent of the disaster will determine the level of response.

Communication. The most common challenge during disaster recovery is the issue of communicating feedback to the central team in charge of response and recovery. Simply communicating over the phone is simply not enough. Also, apart from getting feedback or updates to the central management, the public must also be updated as to the recovery status of the organization.

Secondary Assessment. Apart from the initial assessment, it is imperative to run a thorough and detailed assessment to guide them on the necessary to take.

Reconstitution. Reconstitution is aimed at ensuring a full recovery of operations. For instance, if the organization decides to use an alternate site temporarily, it is necessary to ensure that adequate security measures are put in place to guarantee the safety of their clients but in the meantime, a salvage team will continue working on the primary site. Once the primary site is back to its full capacity, all activities on the alternate site will be channeled back to the primary site.

How to Develop A BCP/DRP

The template of the National Institute of Standards and Technologies Contingency Planning Guide for Federal Information Systems (NIST SP800-34) is recommended when designing a BCP/DRP.

Below are some major steps organizations could adopt:

Project Initiation. To successfully design an effective BCP or DRP, you need to define the scope of the project and all the parties involved must carefully examine it and agree on it.

Conduct BIA. Business Impact Assessment is a tool that organizations employ to assess effect or impact of a disruption on an IT business. BIA will help the management to be able to determine and prioritize certain IT system(s) as well as components. Thus, during the design of BCP/DRP, the management will make better contingency plans for such components. Therefore, any disruption to any of those top priority systems or components will be disastrous to the organization. With BIA, a project manager can estimate the MTD (Maximum Tolerable Downtime) for each IT component. This will determine the response of the disaster management team i.e. if it is a top priority response or not.

Identifying Critical Assets. This collection of top priority IT assets are critical to the smooth running of the organization and as such, they must have the best DRP/BCP.

Determine the Maximum Tolerable Downtime (MTD). The MTD is used to determine how long a business can continue before it feels the impact of a crisis and thus, it is a key component of the BIA.

There are two components of MTD: Recovery Time Objective and Work Recovery Time

Failure and Recovery Metrics. Certain metrics can be implemented to estimate the rate of the system's failure and how long the system remains in that condition, as well as how long it will take the system to fully recover. Such metrics includes:

- *Recovery Point Objective (RPO).* This is an estimate of the total amount of information loss that occurred due to system failure. This can be used to determine how much data loss an organization can afford or bear. For instance, if data is backed up weekly every Friday evening but a system failure occurred a few hours before then, it simply means the company's RPO value = 1 week.

The RPO, therefore, is the maximum amount of work or data loss at a given time due to an unexpected event.

- *Mean Time Between Failures (MTBF).* This is a quantitative measure of the time it will take a new or repaired system to run before it fails. MTBF is usually determined by the manufacturer of such hardware components.

- *Mean Time To Repair (MTTR).* This is used to measure the time it will take a failed system to recover and become fully functional. MTTR is necessary to ensure continuity.

- *Minimum Operating Requirements (MOR).* MOR refers to the basic requirements in terms of connectivity and environmental conditions needed by each IT asset or component to operate. With the MOR of each component, if there is any case of disruption in the future, the IT experts will be able to determine if a particular component will still function despite limited resources (or under an emergency environment).

Identify Preventive Controls. These are preventive measures that are designed to prevent or reduce the chances of disruptive incidences. For instance, the cooling system in computer systems help to prevent overheating and possible system failure.

Recovery Strategy

After determining the BIA, the team in charge of BCP will be able to determine the MTD. Also, with all these metrics at hand, including the RTO and RPO, it is possible for the BCP team to design a strategic recovery process.

Redundant Site. Redundant sites can also be called an alternative or a backup site. Just like the primary site, a redundant site receives real-time data and can be used temporarily as the main site once there is a system failure or a disruptive event that has affected the primary site without the end user noticing any difference in service quality. The only disadvantage of operating a redundant site is that it is very expensive to maintain.

Hot Site. This is similar to a redundant site except that it consists of more sophisticated, high tech computers as well as utilities and enables prompt resumption of critical operations of an organization in the shortest possible time after major disaster. The turn-over could even be less than an hour.

Warm Site. These sites are somewhat related to a hot site in terms of high-tech computer hardware except that it does not receive data but rather depends on data from other systems.

Cold Site. These sites are the cheapest to maintain but take a very long period of time to fully recover after a disruptive event. For instance, new hardware will be purchased or shipped from the manufacturer. With cold sites, MTD could be estimated in weeks or months rather than in days.

Reciprocal/Mutual Agreement. This is a bilateral agreement in which 2 separate organizations agree to share their resources in case any of them suffers from a disaster. This agreement is documented and kept for a rainy day.

Mobile Site. These are fully equipped data centers within a towable trailer and can be moved easily in case primary centers are damaged by disaster such as fire, flood, etc. Mobile has well equipped anti-fire protection as well as other physical security system. The trailer may be towed to the desired site when needed and launched online.

Other Related Plans

Apart from the DRP plan which falls under BCP we have:

Continuity of Operations Plan. COOP illustrates steps to be taken during a disaster for continued production to be ensured. For instance, a staff could be transferred to another site that just experienced a disaster and is still under recovery.

Business Recovery Plan (BRP). Business recovery/resumption plan is a protocol that shows appropriate steps that will lead to the full restoration of business activities after a disaster. If an alternate site was used during the disruption, BRP may involve the transfer of operations to the repaired site (the main site).

BRP can only be utilized after the COOP has been completed.

Continuity of Support Plan (COSP). COSP focuses on how IT applications and systems can be supported. It can be referred to as an IT Contingency Plan, showing that IT is more important than the actual business support.

Cyber-Incident Response Plan (CRP). CRP is designed to address cyber-related events such as trojan horses, computer viruses, worms, etc. for instance, a worm that is coded to disrupt the network or crash the entire systems.

Occupant Emergency Plan (OEP). OEP focuses on the safety of the staff (not IT-focused) within an office facility during an event that could be harmful to the health and general wellbeing of the personnel, or the environment, for example, during an earthquake, a fire outbreak, robbery attack, a medical emergency, etc. It contains the evacuation and safety drills (such as a fire drill) that could save lives during an emergency.

Crisis Management Plan. The crisis management plan is designed to guide the management on what steps to take and how to effectively manage a crisis. It ensures that the management protects the life as well as the safety of each member of staff in the event of a disaster.

Crisis Communications Plan (CCP). The CMP is a communication plan that contains the guidelines on how to pass information to the staff and the general public in case there is a disaster.

After a disaster, a lot of bad news or misinformation will be circulated, hence the need for an official news report directly from the affected organization through the public relations office or a top official.

Call Trees

A call tree is designed to make it possible for an organization to easily communicate with the staff when there is an emergency. This is done by assigning a group of individuals to a top manager who is responsible for reaching those under his care. For instance, the chairman could disseminate information through the managers; the managers will reach out to the supervisors and the supervisors in turn to the staff. After reaching the staff, feedbacks must flow backward in the same manner until it gets back to the chairman.

Keep in mind that during an emergency, phone lines may not be easily accessible, it may be damaged or too congested, and hence, the call tree must contain an alternative means of disseminating information.

Emergency Operations Center (EOC)

The EOC is an emergency post that is set up during or immediately after a crisis. The locating depends on the resources at the disposal of each organization. The EOC for some well-established organizations may be located some distance away from the danger zone to ensure the safety of the staff.

Backups & Availability

The most important reason for using backups is to be able to recover saved data after an emergency. Therefore, it is necessary to review the recovery process for each backup solution. It is recommended that the backup plan should include an offsite storage facility where vital backup data could be stored. The offsite location should, however, must be easily accessible so that the saved media can be transferred to the point where it is needed for recovery.

Hardcopy Data

Hardcopy data are those written on paper and does not require computer processing. Hardcopy data is very useful when there is a disruptive event that affects all the computer systems as well as disrupting the power supply after complications like an earthquake.

Electronic Backups

This is electronically archived data that one could retrieve after a disaster. The choice of backup plan depends on the resources of the organization such as connectivity, size of data to be stored, and most importantly, the goal of the organization. It is important to test the recovery potential of your electronic backups before a disaster to know the recovery capacity.

Full Backups. This involves backing up every single data of the organization on a backup storage. Although this process is time-consuming, it ensures the safety of vital information.

Incremental Backups. As the name implies data is backed up incrementally after an incremental or a full backup.

Differential Backups. This is similar to the incremental backups except that this method selects which data would be restored. For instance if there is loss of data after Tuesday (from the previous example) what is required is:

- The last full backup from Sunday.

- The backup from Tuesday.

Tape Rotation Techniques. One of the most popular tape rotation techniques is known as "First In, First Out" (FIFO) OR ROUND ROBIN. If for instance, an IT firm performs full backup daily on 21 rewritable disks, it means the disk will only be able to backup data for just three weeks. Thus, if data is lost after the third week, there will be no means of restoring the lost data.

To overcome this challenge, the "Grandfather-Father-Son (GFS)" method could be employed. All the disks are divided into three groups:

The Son: 7 daily disks - once a week, a Son disk becomes a Father disk.

The Father: 4 weekly disks - after 5 weeks, it becomes the Grandfather disk.

The Grandfather: 12 monthly disks

After trying this method for a year, one could get data from the last seven days, four weeks, and twelve months.

Electronic Vaulting. This involves the use of electronic transmitters from a primary site to an offsite repository. There are dozens of electronic vaulting devices that could be used to transmit and backup bulk data. It is useful when data is backed up hourly or daily.

Remote Journaling. All database transactions can be stored on a remote database journal (a remote site that is far away from the primary site) and may be of help after a database for the recovery of the lost database. Database journal have checkpoints or snapshot point (points where database data are stored). The checkpoints could be set to save data hourly. Thus, if the database is compromised (at the primary site) 30 min after the last checkpoint, the loss could be restored by checking the last checkpoint (that was sent to the remote site) before the compromise and then continuing to save subsequent data transactions from that checkpoint.

Database Shadowing. This method ensures prompt recovery of data compared to the remote journaling. As the name suggests, two or more identical databases (shadows) are used and simultaneously updated. Assuming two shadow databases are used, one will be at the primary site, while the other will be offsite.

DRP Testing, Training, and Awareness

After designing their DRP, most organizations make a common mistake of not testing the already designed DRP/BCP, not training their staff on how to handle certain crises, and not facilitating general awareness programs. Most DRPs are abandoned on the shelf where they gather dust until there is a crisis and this may be disastrous.

There are some important points to keep in mind about a DRP:

1. A DPR needs to be updated continually amending it as much as possible to ensure efficient recovery after a crisis. A DPR is completed rather it is an on-going process.

2. During the creation of a DRP, there is a possibility of making mistakes which might only be detected during testing. These mistakes, if not corrected, might make recovery challenging hence the need for regular testing and updates.

3. Also, all members of staff need to be familiar with certain complex operations that were designed by top administrators. During a crisis, the administrator(s) might not be available to execute some complex procedures. Hence, the need for all staff to be overly familiar with the procedures stated on the DRP.

4. Special emphasis should be laid on:

   - The role of the general user in the DRP.

- Personnel safety as well as business operations during a disaster.

Test Your DRP.

A DRP cannot be said to be viable unless it has been tested and found to efficiently recover lost data. Change is a constant factor in every organization, thus, if any changes or replacements are made to either a software or hardware component, the DPR also need to be adjusted accordingly.

Review Your DRP

After compiling the DRP, it is imperative to read through it to be sure it is complete and it covers every aspect. Review is a key step in DRP testing and is usually carried out by those who invented the scheme and every member of the team is required to go through it to be sure it is error-free and complete.

Read-Through

This is a form of checklist testing that ensures that all the important components necessary for an efficient and successful recovery are available at all times in case of a disaster. For instance, the tapes required for backup at a remote site should be continually updated to make sure the latest information or data is backed up.

Tabletop or Walkthrough

Walkthrough is usually performed along with the read-through (checklist) testing of the tabletop or walkthrough exercise. This simply means that the team will perform a surface review of the DRP structured manner without digging deep in order to detect any obvious omissions before carrying out an in-depth review (or a read-through).

Simulation Test/Walkthrough Drill

This stage takes us a step further beyond the tabletop exercise. A real-life crisis is simulated which and the team members are expected to test the procedures outlined in the DRP. At first, a minor crisis is simulated and if handled successfully, a more complex crisis will be created.

Partial & Complete Business Interruption

As the name suggests, there is either a partial or complete interruption of the organization's critical business activities at the primary site during the testing exercise. This is the highest form of all DRP tests. When business activities are interrupted at the primary site, the alternate facility will be leveraged on. This type of test is usually carried out by organizations that practice full redundant or load-balance operations.

Continued DRP/BCP Maintenance

Even after testing, training, and implementing the DRP/BCP plan, it is still necessary for IT firms to update the information no matter how small the changes made are. This calls for the need for all professionals to adapt to the ever-changing world of information technology.

Change Management

This has to do with keeping a record of all the changes that occur within an organization. This includes documenting all formal approval for tangible changes as well as keeping track of the outcomes of the completed change. All of these must be reported and kept safely.

BCP & DRP Mistakes

BCP & DRP are the last resorts and final hope of an organization. Failure of these two components could lead to complete failure of the business.

It is, therefore, the duty of the BCP team to ensure that no mistakes are made during the planning process. An honest appraisal of the BCP will help the team to correct or avoid such mistakes.[29]

Specific BCP & DRP Model

There are a number of confusing terminologies associated with various BCP/DRP models. However, below is a list of recommended BCP/DRP frameworks:

NIST- SP 800-34. The National Institute of Standards and Technology (NIST) Publication 800-34 Rev. 1 contains the Contingency Planning Guide for Federal Information Systems.

ISO/IEC-27031. The ISO/IEC-27031 is one of the latest guidelines from the ISO 27000 series. It contains guidelines regarding BCP.

British Standards Institution (BSI)-25999 & ISO 22301

BSI: The BS-25999 is made up of two parts:

- Part 1: This contains:

    o The Code of Practice,

---

[29] Syed Ubaid Ali jafri - CISSP Exam Guide by Eric Conrad,Seth Misenar. (2019). Retrieved from http://docslide.us/education/syed-ubaid-ali-jafri-cissp-exam-guide-by-eric-conradseth-misenar.html

o   Provides business continuity management,

o   And the best practice recommendations.

- Part 2: This provides specific requirements for the BCMS (Business Continuity Management System) and these are based on the best BCM practices.

The ISO 22301:2012 has replaced BS-25999-2 which is the Societal security—Business continuity management systems-Requirements. Soon, the ISO 22301 will also replace the initial British BS 25999-2 and leverage on the standard and the success of the fundamentals system.

The BS ISO 22301 contains specific requirements that are necessary for the establishment & effective management of a BCMS by any organization, irrespective of size or type. The BSI suggests that every organization should have a system or backup plan ready to prevent excessive waste of time and loss of productivity in the event of a disaster.

The Business Continuity Institute (BCI)

The BCI released a 6-step GPG (Good Practice Guideline), which was last updated in 2013.

"The GPG represents the trending global reasoning in good business and are also an independent body of knowledge for good business continuity practice globally."

Chapter Eight

Software Development Security

All over the world, there has been a sudden increase in the development and use of software. Everywhere we go, we find one device or another that makes use of software such as computers, phones, cars, television, video games, etc.

One major challenge we face is the tendency of software programmers to make mistakes which could be very costly. For instance, if a car that is controlled by fly-by-wire systems connected to the internet is hacked, it means the hacker will be in total control of the vehicle and could cause harm to the occupant.

Thus, there is a greater need for software developers to come up with robust & secure software which are reliable. Let us now discuss some fundamentals of programming as well as various computer languages, vulnerabilities of software, etc.

Concept of Programming

Machine Code, Source Code, & Assemblers

Machine code: This is the language that the computer understands and the form in which the CPU (central processing unit) processes information. Machine codes are in binary using a series of 0s & 1s which when combined in a particular manner will give specific instructions to the CPU.

Source code: This is a programming language command written in text that is understandable by humans and which are later translated into machine codes (binary) before the CPU can execute the coded command/instruction.

There are, however, high-level languages written in English for example 'printf' = print formatted.

Assembly language: This language is coded in short forms such as the use of mnemonics, to give instructions or instance: "DIV," (division), "SUB" (subtract), "ADD", etc. They are known as low-level languages and will require an assembler to convert the assembly language into a machine language. Also, a disassembler can be used to convert the machine language back to an assembly language.

Compilers, Interpreters, & Bytecode

Both compilers and interpreters perform the same function but use different approaches. A compiler such as Basic will compile a source code from the beginning to the end before converting it into a machine code. An interpreter (such as shell code) however will be converting the source code into machine codes line by line each time you run the program. Another example of an interpreted code is the Java Bytecode which operates as an intermediary. First, source codes are converted from the source codes to the Bytecode before they are further converted into machine codes by a Java virtual machine which is an independent platform before it can run on the CPU.

138

Computer Aided Software Engineering (CASE)

CASE utilizes other programs to facilitate the creation and maintenance of other software computer programs. CASE has been of great assistance to programmers.

Basically, we have 3 types of CASE software:

- **Tools:** performs one specific task during the production of software.

- **Workbenches:** it combines several tools into one application thus supporting more than one software process.

- **Environments:** This is a collection of tools (or a workbench) and can support all or part of software production activities.

Commonly used CASE components include: object-oriented languages, 4th-generation (4G) computer languages, etc.

Types of Publicly Released Software

After writing a software program designed for public consumption, it can either be released with/without the source code under different licenses.

Open Source & Closed Source Software

- **Closed Source Software:** As the name implies, the source code is hidden while the software is released only in executable form. Examples include Microsoft Windows 10, Oracle etc.

- **Open Source Software:** In contrast to the closed source code, the source codes for this software are published and released to the public. Examples are Linux, Apache web server etc.

- **Proprietary Software:** These are protected by patent or copyright laws as they are intellectual properties of other programmers.

Free Software, Shareware, & Crippleware

- **Free software:** This term has different meanings to different individuals. Some are of the opinion that free means they are free to modify the software (referred to as libre as in liberty) while others feel it means users have access to use the application without paying for it (referred to as gratis).

- **Shareware:** Simply means the user is licensed to have access to the software for a limited period of time (for instance 30 days) after which the user will be required to pay a fee to renew their license.

- **Crippleware:** These come in a partially locked format and users are required to pay a fee to unlock the software in order to have access to its full functionality.

Methods of Application Development

The increasing dependence on software programs as well as the stiff competition among software programmers has facilitated the need for collaboration and team spirit among developers. Therefore, there is a need for coordinated project-based management, a structured project model, goals, objectives, team communication, frequent evaluation, and reporting of progress made so far; as well as the final outcome reporting.

Waterfall Model

This is a stepwise model in which developers complete a step and move to the next. This model could either be a modified model or an unmodified model.

Modified Waterfall Model: This allows a developer the opportunity to go back to a previous step in case there is an error that needed to be corrected.

Unmodified Waterfall model: Once the developer moves to the next step, he cannot step backward for validation or verification.

Sashimi Model

This model is coined from a Japanese meal that consists of slices of raw fish. It can be seen as a modification of the waterfall model and can also be called sashimi waterfall. It was modeled after the hardware design of Fuji-Xerox.

Agile Software Development

This software was developed to overcome the challenges encountered using rigid software models like the waterfall models. Agile utilizes models such as Scrum & XP. Agile is a collection of modern concepts such as improved flexibility, prompt turnaround with little achievements, strong team communication, and more customer engagements.

Scrum. Scrum was developed as an Agile model and the name was derived from the sport of rugby. The newly developed game by Ikujiro and Takeuchi was designed to supersede the former approach of waterfall model which was more like a relay race in which after a team completes a task, they hand it over to the next team. According to them, they would say "stop the marathon and play rugby". In the game of rugby, the ball can be thrown back and forth among the team members. This simply means that the next team doesn't need to wait till the other team completes their task, rather they could joggle tasks amongst themselves. This method was later named by Peter DeGrace (of the sashimi design) as the Scrum and he described it in relation to software creation and design.

- The Scrums = small units of developers (known as the Scrum Team).

- The Scrum Master = a senior member of the organization (the coach for the team), and he gives his support for the Scrum Team.

- The owner = the voice of the business unit.

This approach was necessary if an organization was to stay competitive and meet market demands.

Extreme Programming (XP). Extreme programming is also designed using an Agile development method. This method requires pairs of programmers that work on a specific detail of the product. There is also high degree of customer participation.

XP improves software development in 5 important ways:

- **Communication:** They communicate often with co-programmers as well as customers.

- **Simplicity:** The designs are kept simple and neat.

- **Respect:** They earn the respect of their customers by delivering the product promptly and implementing suggestions.

- **Courage:** They develop the courage to try something new.

- **Feedback:** Test of the product starts from the first day and feedback is gathered.

XP main activities include:

1. **Planning:** This involves certain details such as the product specifications and time it will take to complete the software development.

2. **Paired programming:** Teamwork in pairs.

3. **4-hour workweek:** The assumed timing from the planning stage should be good enough so as to determine the total hours that will be required for the completion of the project. It will also help the team to know if working overtime will be necessary.

4. **Customer involvement:** The client will always be around to monitor the project carefully.

5. **Detailed test procedures:** This is often referred to as unit tests.

Spiral

This method is designed to minimize error as much as possible. As the name suggests, smaller tasks are carried out first and gradually, there is an outward expansion to more complex tasks. Each stage is however repeated before moving on to the next task, and also, a risk analysis is carried out as a way of detecting any fault in the development process thereby mitigating the overall risk. Also, any of the above-mentioned methods could be implemented at any of the stage, for instance the modified waterfall, sashimi, etc.

Rapid Application Development (RAD)

RAD is developed to meet the increase in demand in the world of software development within the shortest possible time by making use of back-end database, prototypes, etc. In this method, the customers are also very much involved.

System Development Life Cycle (SDLC)

SDLC, also known as the system life cycle, is widely used by various IT companies, and its primary aim is to ensure the security of a software development system.

Integrated Product Teams (IPT)

IPT is an integration of multidisciplinary individuals involved in the entire life-cycle of the project such as those in charge of design, production, testing and evaluation, shipment, and other activities necessary for the success of the project including the customer.

IPT is an agile method and the traditional hierarchical procedure in which top management gives instructions that are not followed by the IPT. In IPT, senior management is very much involved in the entire process.

Software Escrow

This process involves an agreement between three parties:

- The software vendor,

- The customer,

- And a neutral party who stores the source code of the software.

This agreement is reached primarily by the customer and the vendor as a way of protecting the source code. The vendor might want to keep the source code secret while the customer might fear that the source code could be lost (or orphaned) if there is an incident. Thus, the third party stores the code as a backup.

Code Repository Security

Code repository could either be owned by the developer or by a third party such as *GitHub. The most important thing is that the security of saved source codes must be guaranteed.

3rd parties raise additional security concerns and provides additional security controls such as:

1. Security of the system

2. File system and backups

3. Maintaining security

4. Safety of credit card

5. Secure communications

6. Operational security

145

7. Staff access

8. Software protection

*(http://www.github.com)

Security of Application Programming Interfaces

API is an application to allows communication with other applications or databases, networks or operating systems. For instance, Google Maps API can integrate third-party content, such as a school that falls under a certain area on Google Maps.

Software Change & Configuration Management

Software Change Management: This provides a model for managing changes made to softwares during the process of development, maintenance, and when they are outdated. Certain organizations consider this process a discipline.

Configuration Management: This can track changes made to a specific part of the software such as changes made to a content management system, specific settings within the software, etc.

In broader terms, change management tracks changes made across the whole software development program. Configuration management and change management are both designed to protect sensitive information when changes are made and to ensure that such changes take place orderly.

DevOps

DevOps is an agile programming method (such as Scrum and Sashimi) that involves the development and operation of software. In this cycle, the developer is fully involved in the entire process.

146

Traditional methods of software development separated the developer from the production team. The quality assurance (QA) team acts as an intermediary between both of them. After developing the software, the QA team will tests it to confirm if it is functional and if it can be mass produced before handing over to the production team. DevOps, therefore, bridges the gap between the developers and the production team.

Databases

A database is an array or collection of closely related data where data can easily be modified. It facilitates easy updates (insertions), removal (deletion), inquires (searches), as well as other activities. DBMS (Database Management System) is under the control of an administrator and it can be used in ensuring access control and database security. SQL (Structured Query Language) are used to search for information on a database.

When multiple databases are used, there are higher chances of compromising the integrity as well as the confidentiality of the stored data.

Foreign Keys

This refers to a key on a database table that is similar to a primary key on a parent database table.

Database Normalization

This ensures normalization that the data on a database table is consistent, organized, and logically accurate. Normalization eliminates redundancy of data and enhances the availability & integrity of the database.

Database Views

Database views refer to the results obtained from querying or searching through a database table that may be queried; the results of a query are called a database view.

Database Query Languages

Database query languages consist of a minimum of two commands:

1. Data definition language (DDL) functions include: creating tables and modifying and deleting tables.

2. Data manipulation language (DML) functions: to query and update previously saved tables.

Object-Oriented Databases

Databases traditionally contain passive data, however, object-oriented databases combine functions (code) and data in an object-oriented framework.

Database Integrity

The integrity of all data on a database must be ensured in order to avoid unauthorized alterations of stored data. Simultaneous attempt to modify data is one of the major challenges that have been noticed to affect data database integrity.

Shadowing and Database Replication

Shadowing: This is similar to a replicated database but the only differences are that all changes made to the primary database will affect all replicated databases, and the clients cannot alter data or make changes to it as they do not have access to the shadow (all data

148

modifications can only be made by the primary administrator, it is one way).

Database Replication: Although replicating a database on multiple servers ensures that all data saved can be retrieved in case the primary database becomes compromised. However, the raises questions regarding the integrity of the information on the database.

A replica of a database is exactly like a live database, and allows simultaneous modification by clients on the replicated database. To overcome the challenge of integrity compromise, a 2-phase or multiphase commit can be used.

Data Repository/Warehouse and Data Mining

Data Warehouse: A data warehouse contains a large collection of data; the stored data could be as large as multiple terabytes (1024 gigabytes) or petabytes (1024 terabytes). Thus, there is a constant need for large storage capacity with optimum performance that allows easy access to stored data.

Data Mining: This is used to search through stored data by searching for specific patterns such as signs of fraud. Credit card companies manage the largest data warehouses in the world and they track billions of online transactions yearly as fraudulent transactions cost them millions of dollars. It will be difficult if not impossible for humans to track all these transactions, hence the need to monitor transactions using data mining which can separate the fraud signals from random noise.

One of the patterns tracked is the use of a single card to carry out multiple transactions simultaneously in different states or countries. If this is detected, the system will flag a violation signal and the card owner would be contacted immediately on the phone or the card would be suspended.

Object-Oriented Programming (OOP)

With OOP, certain functions (such as sending or receiving a message) are hidden within an object (also known as a black box). This protects the data of the users from being compromised.

Cornerstone Object Oriented Programming Concepts (COOPC)

COOPC also uses objects, but it is more complex than the OOP. It consists of the following characteristics, each of which will be using an object called ADDY (function: addition of two integers)

Inheritance: ADDY or addition inherits its function from normal mathematical operations (regarded as the Parent)

Delegation: If a function which it does not perform is requested for, it can delegate it to other objects that can perform that function.

Polymorphism: Allows ADDY to join two strings together, for example integer+integer.

Polyinstantiation: This function is necessary when you input two objects that have the same name but perform different functions, i.e. multiple instances (polyinstantiation).

Poly-instantiation can be used to hide top profile data.

Object Request Brokers (ORBs)

These are search engines used to locate objects. They serve as application interphase and connect one program to the other. Examples of commonly used ORBs are:

- CORBA
- DCOM
- COM

Assessing the Effectiveness of Software Security

After completing a software design, it is necessary to test the software for its ability to perform the expected function(s) as well as to detect any fault or vulnerability which could lead to system compromise of the entire program. It is also necessary to test the software as a means of measuring its effectiveness and see areas that needs improvement.

Software Vulnerabilities

No one is perfect, and that includes programmers who are also prone to making mistakes when developing a program. Despite many years of experience, mistakes are bound to occur. Although, the number of mistakes per line can be reduced, it can never be completely avoided.

Some common types of software vulnerabilities include:[30]

1. **Hardcoded Credentials:** This occurs when the programmer forgets to erase backdoor username or passwords used while developing the code.

---

[30] Syed Ubaid Ali jafri - CISSP Exam Guide by Eric Conrad,Seth Misenar. (2019). Retrieved from http://docslide.us/education/syed-ubaid-ali-jafri-cissp-exam-guide-by-eric-conradseth-misenar.html

2. **Buffer Overflow:** The programmer fails to perform variable bounds check. This can be used to insert and run shellcodes such as UNIX/LINUX Shell or Microsoft Windows cmd.exe. to prevent this, use secure application developments that perform bounds checking.

3. **SQL Injection:** When the front-end server is used to manipulate a back-end SQL due to programmers mistakes.

4. **Directory Path Traversal:** Moving from the base of a web server (such as www) into a file system just by referencing directories such as "/".

5. **PHP Remote File Inclusion (RFI):** This can be done by modifying the usual PHP URLs as well as the variables for instance as "http://fine.example.com?file=readme.txt" and adding additional remote content like http://fine.example.com?file=http://bad.example.com/bad.php1 4

6. **Time of Check (TOC)/Time of Use (TOU) race conditions:** The attacker tries to make certain changes in the normal condition by capitalizing on a change in the state of the operating system.

7. **Cross-Site Scripting (XSS) and Cross-Site Request Forgery (CSRF or XSRF):** Takes advantage of the use of a third-party web scripting (for example a JavaScript) within a trusted context of a secured site.

CSRF or XSRF depends on the static content or a redirect from the third-party within the security context of a secured site. The main difference is that XSS will execute scripts within a trusted context.

1. **Privilege Escalation:** This occurs when a program is poorly coded giving an attacker with limited access additional access.

2. **Backdoors:** These are shortcuts that allows an attacker to bypass all security checkpoints (for example - username/password) that were put in place to protect the system from being compromised.

Disclosure

This describes what takes place after a vendor conducts a vulnerability check on the software and discovers certain loopholes. Disclosure can either be:

- **Full disclosure:** In which the vulnerability details are made public.

- **Responsible disclosure:** In which the vulnerability details are kept private until necessary adjustments are made and are available before informing the public.

Software Capability Maturity Model (CMM)

It was designed and developed by the Software Engineering Institute, Carnegie Mellon University. It can be used in improving software development process as well as to evaluate the maturity framework of softwares.

Acceptance Testing

According to ISTQB (International Software Testing Qualifications Board), acceptance testing is defined as "a formal testing process conducted with respect to client's needs, requirements, and specification."

This testing is conducted to ensure that software designs meet up with the various requirements, of a user, client, contract, or compliance principles.

Commercial Off-The-Shelf Software (COTS)

Vendor claims are more readily verifiable for Commercial Off-The-Shelf (COTS) Software. If you wish to purchase COTS, do not rely on information from the vendors but rather, conduct a general test by comparing it with a product that meets the basic requirements.

Custom Developed Third-Party Applications (CDTPA)

A better alternative that can be used in place of COTS is the use of CDTPA. CDTPA provides both extra benefits as well as extra risks than COTS. It is necessary to obligate security considerations by ensuring that there is a contractual or service level agreement (SLA) when a third-party development firm is involved and never assuming that security issues will be considered during the development. The issue of security should be carefully discussed and ironed out before going into contract with the third party. Certain questions that require serious considerations include:

- What will happen if the vendor runs out of business?

- What will happen if a key feature is missing?

- How easy will it be to find an internal or third-party support for the vendor's products?

154

Bibliography

Andress, J. (2011). The basics of information security. Waltham, MA: Syngress.

CISSP – Adventures in the programming jungle. (2019). Retrieved from https://adriancitu.com/category/certification/cissp/page/2/

Commanments_of_Computer_Ethics.htm.

Common Cryptographic Algorithms. (2019). Retrieved from http://web.deu.edu.tr/doc/oreily/networking/puis/ch06_04.htm

Conrad, E., Misenar, S., & Feldman, J. (2017). Domain 1. Eleventh Hour CISSP®, 1-32. doi: 10.1016/b978-0-12-811248-9.00001-2

Downnard, I. (2002). Public-key cryptography extensions into Kerberos. IEEE Potentials, 21(5), 30-34. doi: 10.1109/mp.2002.1166623

Fundamentals of Information Systems Security/Access Control Systems - Wikibooks, open books for an open world. (2019). Retrieved from https://en.wikibooks.org/wiki/Fundamentals_of_Information_Systems_Security/Access_Control_Systems

Garfinkel, S., Schwartz, A., & Spafford, G. (2003). Practical Unix and Internet security. Beijing: O'Reilly.

Grasdal, M. (2017). Microsoft® U.S. National Security Team White Paper. Retrieved from http://download.microsoft.com/download/d/3/6/d36a0a81-6aa8-4ff4-835e-9a017df1f036/SecureCollaborationForProfSvcFirms.doc

https://docslide.us/education/syed-ubaid-ali-jafri-cissp-exam-guide-by-eric-conradseth-misenar.html

Information Asset and Security Classification Procedure - University of Southern Queensland. (2019). Retrieved from https://policy.usq.edu.au/documents/13931PL

Information Security Chapter 5 Flashcards | Quizlet. (2019). Retrieved from https://quizlet.com/37179514/information-security-chapter-5-flash-cards/

Information Security Risk Management. (2019). Retrieved from http://isoconsultantpune.com/information-security-risk-management/

Jorrigala, Vyshnavi, "Business Continuity and Disaster Recovery Plan for Information Security" (2017). Culminating Projects in Information Assurance. 44. http://repository.stcloudstate.edu/msia_etds/44

Kabay, M. (2006). Introduction to Computer Crime. Retrieved from http://www.mekabay.com/overviews/crime.pdf

Marco, H., Ripoll, I., de Andrés, D., & Ruiz, J. (2014). Security through Emulation-Based Processor Diversification. Emerging Trends In ICT Security, 335-357. doi: 10.1016/b978-0-12-411474-6.00021-9

Online. 1992. Accessed 4 March 2019 from www.brook.edu/its/cei/overview/Ten_

RAID level 0, 1, 5, 6 and 10 | Advantage, disadvantage, use. (2019). Retrieved from https://www.prepressure.com/library/technology/raid

Syed Ubaid Ali jafri - CISSP Exam Guide by Eric Conrad,Seth Misenar. (2019). Retrieved from http://docslide.us/education/syed-ubaid-ali-jafri-cissp-exam-guide-by-eric-conradseth-misenar.html

The Computer Ethics Institute. "The 10 Commandments of Computer Ethics." CEI

The OSI Model – What It Is; Why It Matters; Why It Doesn't Matter. (2019). Retrieved from http://www.tech-faq.com/osi-model.html

The XOR Cipher - HackThis!!. (2019). Retrieved from https://www.hackthis.co.uk/articles/the-xor-cipher

Types of Fires and Extinguishing Agents – The Fire Equipment Manufacturers' Association. (2019). Retrieved from https://www.femalifesafety.org/types-of-fires.html

von Solms, B. (2005). Information Security governance: COBIT or ISO 17799 or both?. Computers & Security, 24(2), 99-104. doi: 10.1016/j.cose.2005.02.002

What is Secondary Memory? - Definition from Techopedia. (2019). Retrieved from https://www.techopedia.com/definition/2280/secondary-memory

Wilson, S. (2007). The FCC Hearing at Stanford. Legal Research Paper Series, 21. Retrieved from https://law.stanford.edu/wp-content/uploads/2015/07/wilsons-rp21.pdf

Printed in Great Britain
by Amazon